RESILIENCE

STRENGTH TO OVERCOME LIFE'S SETBACKS AND STORMS

JOE GORMAN

To the beloved of God at
Golden Church of the Nazarene in Colorado
Faithful friends and fertile soil in which resilience could take root,
grow, and bear fruit in my own life
(1989–2010)

CONTENTS

PREFACE

How ironic. Here I am writing a book on resilience, and I myself have been struggling to be resilient. During the writing of this book, I've experienced several life-shaking events. Our beloved five-year-old golden retriever, Max, died suddenly. As I was hitting my stride on the last lap of writing, I had to have back surgery. The surgery itself went well, and I was feeling strong and ready to add more movement to my daily life when an infection began to brew, which required four weeks of antibiotics. I eventually had two more minor surgical procedures to help the infection heal. Four weeks on a wound VAC followed.

During this time, I continued to teach my full schedule of university classes. In college there are no substitute teachers! The semester kept rolling on, and I showed up as best as I could, but I struggled to keep up with seven classes. It felt like the semester would never end. If this were not enough, my daughter, Annie, had elbow surgery. Then my wife, Shelly, had surgery to remove a benign brain tumor. During this stormy season, my emotional life often alternated between anger and sadness, with just enough joy sprinkled in to keep me going. And we all struggled through the uncharted waters of the COVID-19 pandemic.

With God's help, I've gotten up each time I've fallen. Practicing habits of prayer, positive self-talk, cultivating gratitude, playing golf, getting adequate sleep, and exercising regularly have helped me stay faithful spiritually, recover physically, and heal emotionally. Experiencing the beauty of creation during daily walks along the river as fall leaves turned golden, short winter days passed into the liveliness of spring, and spring leapt into the long, warm, glorious days of summer have also helped to heal my weary soul.

As we begin our journey through this book, I want you to know that I'm a work in progress. Resilience is not something we become experts at once and for all. Just as with growing in love, resilience is a character trait that we strive and work toward every day of our lives. Sometimes we're prepared for the storms of life; other times we're not. With God's help and that of friends and loved ones, we do the best we can.

My own recent season of struggle has reminded me that the life of Christlike holiness is not one of absolute flawlessness, where we never make mistakes and always get things right. It's about getting up one more time than we fall down. It's persevering "despite a ton of bad luck" (Psalm 116:10, MSG). It's knowing that, because of God's constant love, we always have the landing pad of grace to catch us when we fall. It's keeping our eyes on Jesus rather than on the storms that may be forming on the horizon.

The troubles we encounter often catch us off guard, even though Jesus himself told us we will have trouble. Trouble today. Trouble tomorrow. Count on it. So don't be surprised when trouble comes knocking, he says. Because he has overcome the world, we can too (see John 16:33).

What follows is a cautionary story about resilience.

A Cautionary Tale

In the fall of 1992, Michael Plant, one of the United States' most highly skilled sailors, set out on a solo crossing of the North Atlantic Ocean, from New York to France. Just eleven days after he left New York Harbor, radio contact was lost. A massive search ensued, covering more than two hundred thousand square miles.

Plant was a seasoned sailor, having sailed around the world solo three times. He had sailed through hurricanes and had even survived his yacht capsizing in forty-five-foot swells in the Indian Ocean. He had "repaired a broken mast, fixed a busted generator, [and] repaired his hull after a collision with another vessel off Cape Town."[1] He also had numerous close calls with icebergs. Because of these and other experiences, he knew well the perils of inadequate preparation and lack of constant vigilance on the open sea.

Plant's boat, *Coyote*, was state-of-the-art. *Coyote* was a new boat and largely untested. Plant had taken it out for only a few brief trips before leaving for France. The one concern he had before his trip was that he had not grown familiar enough with the boat.

For pinpoint emergency location, Plant had purchased a Raytheon 406 Emergency Position-indicating Radio Beacon (EPIRB). This beacon is designed to send a signal to a satellite every fifty seconds. This signal is then sent to the National Oceanic and Atmospheric Administration (NOAA), which in turn relays the message to the Coast Guard. In *Coyote*'s case, the Coast Guard never received a notification from NOAA. Later investigation revealed that Plant's EPIRB sent out weak transmission bursts two weeks after leaving New York Harbor. Instead of the four bursts necessary to fix a boat's location, there had been only three. His friends later discovered that, in Plant's haste to leave, he had failed to register his EPIRB with the NOAA—a mistake that may have cost him his life.

Coyote was eventually found, but only after Plant had been lost at sea for thirty-two days. The sixty-foot racing yacht was found capsized, drifting upside down in eight-foot swells. *Coyote*'s eighty-five-foot mast was submerged in the freezing waters,

---

1. E. M. Swift, "Mystery at Sea," *Sports Illustrated Vault*, November 30, 1992, https://vault.si.com/vault/1992/11/30/mystery-at-sea-after-a-massive-sea-and-air-search-the-60-foot-racing-sloop-coyote-was-found-capsized-in-the-north-atlantic-but-the-fate-of-her-skipper-round-the-world-sailor-michael-plant-was-still-unknown. I have drawn primarily from this article in summarizing Plant's fate.

still fully rigged with sails. The boat's hull was intact, its twin rudders operational. Even its carbon-filter keel was still in place. Missing, however, was *Coyote*'s 8,400-pound lead keel bulb. Without an intact keel bulb, there was insufficient counteracting weight to keep the boat upright in a strong wind or severe storm. Without the weight of a keel bulb, no yacht can right itself once it overturns. In order for a sailboat to remain stable and upright in the midst of deep swells and howling winds, there must be more "more weight below the waterline than there is above it. Any violation of this principle of weight distribution means disaster."[2]

No one ever discovered why the 8,400-pound bulb broke away from the keel. Gordon MacDonald asks, "Did *Coyote* hit an underwater object? Some ocean debris? Was there a defect in the boatbuilding process?"[3]

Searchers, upon reaching the overturned boat, found the emergency life raft still inside the ship, halfway inflated, but no sign of Plant. His loss remains a mystery to this day, decades later.

What are some of the lessons that this tragic story raises about resilience?

- Storms come unexpectedly to us all. We cannot escape storms. We can only learn how to weather them.
- Character, like a keel bulb, is often unseen but is completely necessary for enduring the storms of life.
- "'Sub-waterline issues' seem unimportant when seas are calm and winds are favorable. So it's only when the storms hit and something catastrophic happens that we are likely to ask a different set of questions."[4]

---

2. Gordon MacDonald, *The Life God Blesses: Weathering the Storms of Life That Threaten the Soul* (Nashville: Thomas Nelson, 1997), 4. MacDonald's book is the first place I learned of Plant's story.

3. MacDonald, *The Life God Blesses*, 4.

4. MacDonald, *The Life God Blesses*, 11.

- What regular practices help you care for what's below waterline in your life?
- How do you intentionally seek to strengthen your character so you can remain resilient when storms hit?

• Any sea captain will tell you that if you steer a ship just a few degrees this way or that, you will completely alter its trajectory. Over the course of a long journey, it may end up hundreds of miles from where it would have without that slight adjustment.

- What practices help keep you on course spiritually, physically, emotionally, and relationally?

Michael Plant's story highlights the importance of incorporating daily practices into our lives that build resilience and can act as a counterbalance when the storms of life threaten to capsize us. This concept is not meant to add to our already overwhelmed lives. It's meant to help us see that we can take small steps and begin adding micro habits to the lives we already live. Like anything else that nurtures our relationship with God and others, it will take effort and patience. If we forget or get distracted, we can begin again. The point is to alter the compass of our lives just fractions of a degree. Even a small change to our compass can make a world of difference in our final destination.

INTRODUCTION

Resilience

RESILIENCE TIP

Resilient people learn to cultivate Christlike character that will help them weather the storms of life.

> We've been surrounded and battered by troubles, but we're not demoralized; we're not sure what to do, but we know that God knows what to do; we've been spiritually terrorized, but God hasn't left our side; we've been thrown down, but we haven't broken.
>
> —2 Corinthians 4:8–9 (MSG)

> "Sometimes," said the horse.
> "Sometimes what?" asked the boy.
> "Sometimes just getting up and carrying on is brave and magnificent."
> —Charlie Mackesy, The Boy, the Mole, the Fox and the Horse

> These are times in which a genius would wish to live. It is not in the still calm of life, or in the repose of a pacific station, that great characters are formed. The habits of a vigorous mind are formed in contending with difficulties. Great necessities call out great virtues.
> —Abigail Adams to John Quincy Adams, 1780

Life is hard. Sometimes we feel like quitting. How do we respond when life becomes difficult? When marriage seems impossible? When our kids have lost their way? When there are conflicts at church? When we experience unrelenting pain or illness? When our finances are overwhelming? When our jobs are unbearable? What do we do when we feel like we're living life on a treadmill—going faster and faster without going anywhere? How do we persevere? How do we finish well?

This is a book about resilience—about how, with God's help, we can become the kind of people who are able to withstand the setbacks and storms of life. It's been said that authors write the books we ourselves need. That is true for me, both in this book and in my previous book, *Healthy. Happy. Holy: 7 Practices toward a Holistic Life.*[1] Before starting to write this present book, I had grown weary and didn't know how much I needed a book on this topic until I started writing it. I hope you find ideas, stories, encouragement, and courage in these pages to keep loving, to keep hoping, to remain faithful even in difficult times. May we be able to say along with the psalmist, "I stayed faithful, though overwhelmed, and despite a ton of bad luck, despite giving up on the human race, saying, "They're all liars and cheats" (Psalm 116:10–11, MSG).

Most of the lessons I've learned in my life about how to be more resilient have come uninvited. Whatever resilience there is in my life that has taken root has largely been in response to unexpected setbacks. I've tried my best to "make hay while the sun shines," but it's usually when I'm in the eye of the storm that I most carefully pay attention to God. Like many, perhaps, I don't change so much when I see the light but when I feel the heat. I've also learned that the most difficult seasons of life are the ones in which I discover just how deep the love of God and my own character go.

The final race of the 1968 Mexico City Olympics was the marathon. As the last runners were crossing the finishing line,

---

1. I want to encourage you, if you ever write a book, not to have the three words "healthy," "happy," and "holy" in it! People like to ask me, "How are you doing at being healthy, happy, *and* holy?" I think about it like a good baseball player does. If I can get a hit one out of every three at bats, I'm doing very well.

word came in that one more runner was still out there, struggling to finish. Only a few spectators remained as darkness settled on the stadium. The last runner, John Stephen Akhwari of Tanzania, had been injured during the race but had continued to run despite incredible pain. With his injured right knee bandaged, he hobbled the last lap around the stadium and stumbled across the finish line well over an hour behind the winner. As he crossed, those who remained in the stadium went berserk, applauding him as if he had won.

He was later asked, "Why didn't you quit?"

His answer was simple: "My country did not send me five thousand miles to start the race. They sent me five thousand miles to finish the race."[2]

Few of us will ever be Olympians. Nevertheless, God has given each of us a race to run (1 Corinthians 9:24–25). Like Akhwari, we will encounter unforeseen obstacles along the way. We will be tempted to quit. Persevering in the face of overwhelming circumstances is what I call resilience. I find the following definitions of resilience helpful as well.

Dictionary.com: *the power or ability of a material to return to its original form, position, etc., after being bent, compressed, or stretched; elasticity; the ability of a person to adjust to or recover readily from illness, adversity, major life changes, etc.; buoyancy.*[3]

The American Psychological Association: *Resilience is the process and outcome of successfully adapting to difficult or challenging life experiences, especially through mental, emotional, and behavioral flexibility and adjustment to external and internal demands.*[4]

Various synonyms for resilience also come to mind: perseverance, patience, endurance, buoyancy, flexibility, adaptability, elasticity, tenacity, character, courage, steadfastness of spirit, grit,

---

2. A video of Akhwari finishing his Olympic race can be viewed at: https://www.youtube.com/watch?v=k6oW9uYtJnA.

3. https://www.dictionary.com/browse/resilience.

4. *APA Dictionary of Psychology*, "Resilience," https://www.apa.org/topics/resilience.

moxie. Those who are resilient also exhibit many so-called child-ish characteristics: curiosity, wonder, exuberance, teachability, humility, and an always-ready-for-adventure attitude. We will need childlike enthusiasm and openness to all that God desires to teach us on the road to living lives of Christlike character.

Resilient souls finish well. Finishing well doesn't mean we never stumble or fall or that we always get everything exactly right. No matter how fierce the pain or deep the humiliation, resilient ones get back up one more time than they fall down. As the apostle Paul put it, "We often suffer, but we are never crushed. Even when we don't know what to do, we never give up. In times of trouble, God is with us, and when we are knocked down, we get up again" (2 Corinthians 4:8–9, CEV). It's not *where* we finish. It's *that* we finish. "We get up again," Paul says. Like Akhwari, we may stumble, fall, and fail—yet we strain to find the strength to struggle on.

Resilience isn't something we do on our own. We need one another in order to run well the race we've been given. Perhaps you've seen the "pass it on" commercials from The Foundation for a Better Life. One of the most poignant pictures is of young athletes stopping in the middle of the race to help a fallen friend so they can all finish together.[5] What better picture of the Christian life is there than this? As the body of Christ, with each part fulfilling its God-given purpose, we strengthen one another by staying connected, like tendons that connect muscle to bone. Our goal is not to finish first but to finish together. And that takes resilience.

Resilient people weather adversity. We finish what we start. We encourage and train ourselves in stubborn hope. We flex muscles of faith. We trust in God and lean on our companions in Christ. When we fall down, we allow others to dust us off, bandage our wounds, and help us get back to our feet. With grace and mercy, we also help others who have fallen to get back up and continue their race.

---

5. You can find this wonderful video at https://www.passiton.com/inspirational-stories-tv-spots/142-special-athlete.

Resilience isn't a competition. It's not about winning or losing, succeeding or failing. It's about helping someone who's lost their way find hope again. It's persisting in small acts of love even when there are no visible results. It's continuing to lean into faith, hope, and love in spite of setbacks, temptations, trials, pain, failure, or despair.

Resilience is deeply vulnerable. When we're with those who truly love us, we don't need to pretend. In an environment of love and trust, we can truly be our God-created-in-Christ selves. We can dare to tell others what's really going on in our lives. And we can dare to listen to others, offering them a safe place where they too can be their whole selves and hear the voice of love assuring them, "You are my beloved child. Nothing can ever snatch you from my hand" (See John 10:28; Romans 8:35, 37–39).

Resilience is also both gift and craft. Resilience is a fruit of the Spirit's work in us, where God plants seeds of perseverance in the soil of our lives so we can remain standing when the winds of adversity threaten to topple us. But resilience is also a skill we can hone. There are certain practices—what we Wesleyan Christians refer to as "means of grace"—that draw upon the resources of God to strengthen our grit muscles so we can "run with perseverance the race marked out for us" (Hebrews 12:1).[6]

John Wesley believed that growth in Christlikeness was neither automatic nor accidental. None of us wander or stumble into spiritual maturity. We cultivate Christlike character by actively practicing the means of grace. N. T. Wright says something similar: "The qualities of character Jesus and his followers insist on as the vital signs of healthy Christian life don't come about automatically. You have to develop them. You have to work at them."[7] Resilience is a cord of three strands: God's Spirit working

---

6. For those who are not familiar with the term "Wesleyan," it refers to Protestant church traditions that continue to be formed by the life and ministry of eighteenth-century Anglican priest John Wesley, who is considered the founder of the Methodist movement.

7. N. T. Wright, *After You Believe: Why Christian Character Matters* (New York: HarperOne, 2010), 28.

in us (grace), our faithful response to everyday problems (circumstances), and our intentional efforts to grow in Christlike holiness (formative practices). None of us is born pre-loaded with resilience. Resilience grows gradually as we respond to the temptations, trials, setbacks, and failures of a lifetime.

The apostle Paul often refers to the Christian life as a race. In the book of Acts, Paul says, "However, I consider my life worth nothing to me; my only aim is to finish the race and complete the task the Lord Jesus has given me—the task of testifying to the good news of God's grace" (20:24). At the end of Paul's life he tells his protégé in the faith, Timothy: "I have fought the good fight, I have finished the race, I have kept the faith" (2 Timothy 4:7). The race Paul is referring to is not a sprint but a marathon—perhaps even something more like an ultra-marathon.

When I lived in Colorado, I frequently heard about those who ran hundred-mile ultra-marathons in the mountains. I was grateful just to be able to hike up a fourteen-thousand-foot mountain, so running up and down and back up was definitely on this side of impossible for me. As I did some research on ultra-marathons, I was shocked to find out they are run all over the world, often in some of the most arid and elevated places on the planet. These races wend their way through mountains and valleys, twists and turns, night and day, hot and cold, rocks and snakes, with obstacles around every corner. An ultra-marathon is a good image of the kind of life we have set before us.

Resilience is a journey. Some days everything will go right. Other days it will seem the deck is stacked against us. Life is unpredictable and sometimes cruel. What is constant is God's faithfulness. When the winds of adversity howl and the waves rage, it's tempting to take our eyes off God and put them onto our circumstances. Just like the disciples in the boat with a sleeping Jesus, we cry out, "Lord, are we going to drown?"

The disciples were so overwhelmed by the storm that they couldn't even think to ask Jesus to save them. The only thing that occurred to them was to cry out the first thing that came to their minds: "We're going to drown!" (see Mark 4:35–41). This story comforts me because I don't always have the best first response to the storms of life either—or the best second or third response, for that matter. Like the disciples, we may not always know the right words to pray. The only thing we can do in times like these is to cry out, whimper, wail, and groan (see Romans 8:22–27).

My Journey with Depression

When I was in my mid-thirties, I found myself in the clutches of a clinical depression from which I feared I would never escape. I remember all too well how ashamed I was at "allowing" myself to become depressed. Depression felt like weakness and failure to me. I thought at the time that I was the only pastor ever to have experienced depression. I had the unrealistic idea that pastors were always strong, happy, and free of doubt—which of course meant I viewed myself as a failure.

I will talk more fully about my depression in a later chapter, but for now I want to say that, in my journey to crawl out of the pit of despair, one of the most helpful things that happened to me during this time was having to write my doctoral dissertation. During a time when I largely lacked the energy to get out of bed and felt like giving up most days, having a dissertation to write gave me purpose and direction. I realize not everyone would have this response to having such a daunting task hanging over their head while battling depression, but for me at the time it was life-giving. It gave me a track to run on. I may not have been able to figure out what to cook my wife and young children for dinner, but the dissertation work was at least one thing that appeared clear to me.[8]

---

8. In order to keep this book to a readable length, I'm compressing a long period of time with many bouts of hopelessness and despair into a more manageable narrative. For the dissertation I wrote, see Joe Gorman, *The Management and Prevention of*

After starting to take antidepressant medication and undergo counseling, I slowly began to emerge from the deepest dregs of depression. It didn't take long for me to figure out that the most obvious topic in the world for my dissertation was to write about helping pastors—including myself!—manage burnout and depression. So that's what I did. Thankfully, I was able to engage in an academic exercise and work toward healing at the same time. Writing was a lifeline for me. We truly do write the books we ourselves need. What I also discovered during that process is just how many pastors and laypeople suffer from depression. Depression is no respecter of persons. Even faithful, lifelong Christ followers can lose heart and experience deep depression.

As I went about my research, it became crucial for me to know I was not the only one ever to have experienced depression. I needed some heroes of faith, like those in Hebrews 11, to encourage me: *Joe, keep running, don't give up. Your depression will not last forever. We've been there. We felt hopeless at times too. But God is faithful. God will make a way where there seems to be no way. We recovered, and so can you.*

As I studied the psychology and biology of depression, I also began to do some rummaging around in church history. Somewhere along the way I heard rumors that some well-known Christian leaders had also experienced depression. It took some digging because we in the church talk about depression about as much as we talk about our sex lives—which isn't much. It wasn't long before I began to see just how prevalent burnout and depression have been among Christian leaders throughout the centuries, including Martin Luther, J. B. Phillips, William Cowper, Henri Nouwen, Mother Teresa, Charles Spurgeon, Martin Luther King, Jr., and even John Wesley,[9] to name a few.

Burnout and Depression in Pastors, Fuller Theological Seminary, 1999, https://www.proquest.com/openview/4042f4c982d2a4d81135db280940ad35/1?pq-origsite=gscholar&cbl=18750&diss=y.

9. If you are interested in learning more about some of the depressive episodes Wesley went through, see Joe Gorman, "John Wesley in an Age of Melancholy," *Wesleyan Theological*

That these heroes and heroines of faith also experienced depression helped normalize my own experience. It also normalized my humanity. It was a lifeline to discover there was nothing unusual or defective about me. I was simply human. I don't think it's accurate to say that we are "only" human, but it is true that we are *indeed* human. As fragile and frail beings, our lives are a mixture of strength and weakness. We laugh and cry. Rejoice and mourn. Hope and despair. Worship and weep.

The more I read about the history of depression among Christian leaders, the more encouraged I felt. I was not alone. I was a member of a long community of faith that sought to be faithful Christ followers in the midst of sometimes overwhelming seasons of life. Like me, they felt like giving up from time to time. I was not the first or the last to feel this way. As I learned that others had experienced depression yet finished their races well, I began to experience glimmers of hope that I might finish mine as well. The dark, thick fog slowly began to recede. This is one of the reasons I love reading memoirs, biographies, and journals of those whose character was forged in the crucible of incredible obstacles and immense pain. Several who have shaped my own journey toward resilience include Corrie ten Boom, Dietrich Bonhoeffer, Martin Luther King, Jr., John Lewis, Viktor Frankl, Etty Hillesum, Nicholas Wolterstorff, Anthony Ray Hinton, Kate Bowler.

Corrie ten Boom was the only one of her family to survive the Holocaust. The rest of her family was murdered in the Ravensbrück concentration camp. In spite of living through unimaginable horrors, Corrie later wrote several books and spoke of God's presence with her and her sister, Betsie, throughout their time in Ravensbrück. Before Betsie's death in Ravensbrück, she told Corrie, "[We] must tell people what we have learned here. We

---

Journal, 34:2, 1999. If I were writing this article today, the biggest change I would make is to take out the spiritualizing approach I took toward depression. I was still in the early years of my own recovery and had a long journey ahead of me when I wrote this article.

must tell them that there is no pit so deep that [God] is not deeper still. They will listen to us, Corrie, because we have been here."[10]

Dietrich Bonhoeffer, a German pastor and one of the most significant Christian theologians of the twentieth century, was teaching at Union Theological Seminary in the United States during Hitler's rise to power. He could have remained safe and comfortable in his prestigious post, but his understanding of the cost of Christian discipleship compelled him to return to his homeland to resist the spreading menace of Nazism. After returning to Germany, he started a seminary in Finkenvalde to train ministers in the Confessing Church. His goal was to train leaders who would stay faithful to Christ in the midst of the Nazi takeover of churches throughout Germany. Bonhoeffer was involved in a plot to assassinate Hitler that narrowly missed. As a result, he was imprisoned for two years. Even in prison he continued to write to family and friends. One of his most important books, *Letters and Papers from Prison*, came from this time. Bonhoeffer was executed at the Flossenbürg concentration camp on April 9, 1945, less than a month before the Allies liberated Europe. His witness to the cost of following Christ continues to resonate today.

Anthony Ray Hinton was wrongly imprisoned for twenty-eight years for a murder he did not commit. Living in the shadow of death row for most of his years in prison, Hinton often felt hopeless. Lester, his best friend since childhood, drove eight hours one way every Friday night after getting off work to see him for an hour once a week for twenty-eight straight years. Friends like this sustain us in the midst of the deepest hopelessness of our lives. When Hinton had given up hope that he would ever be exonerated, lawyer Bryan Stevenson from the Equal Justice Initiative took on his case. Stevenson was and is a fierce advocate for the underrepresented and wrongly imprisoned. He wrote about his work with the Equal Justice Initiative in his poignant and

---

10. Corrie ten Boom, *The Hiding Place* (Old Tappen, NJ: Fleming H. Revell Company, 1971), 217.

eye-opening book *Just Mercy*. After working more than fifteen years to free Hinton, Stevenson won the right to represent the case before the United States Supreme Court, and in February 2014, the Supreme Court unanimously overturned Hinton's conviction. The state of Alabama, where Hinton had been imprisoned all those years, eventually followed suit, dropping all charges. Hinton was released from prison April 3, 2015. Hinton's faithfulness and Christian witness stand as a living reminder that we too can maintain hope even in the midst of the most hopeless of circumstances.[11]

Martin Luther King, Jr., and John Lewis, both pastors and political activists, gave their lives to advocate for justice in the face of racism, oppression, and often violent opposition.[12]

Kate Bowler is learning to live faithfully with stage-four colon cancer as a college professor, writer, podcaster, wife, and mother.[13]

Nicholas Wolterstorff learned how to go on living after the loss of his twenty-five-year-old son in a mountaineering accident.[14]

Viktor Frankl's ability to imagine life after Auschwitz enabled him to find a reason to endure the daily horrors of concentration camp life and survive conditions that overwhelmed so many others. One of Frankl's most important insights for our purposes are the observations he made about how resilient and not so resilient people fared in Auschwitz: "Even though conditions such as lack of sleep, insufficient food and various mental stresses may suggest that the inmates were bound to react in certain ways, in the final analysis, it becomes clear that the sort of person the prisoner became was the result of an inner decision and not the result of camp influences

---

11. For Hinton's memoir, see Anthony Ray Hinton, *The Sun Does Shine: How I Found Life, Freedom, and Justice* (New York: St. Martin's Griffin, 2018).

12. For a moving biography of Lewis, see Jon Meacham, *His Truth Is Marching On: John Lewis and the Power of Hope* (New York: Random House, 2020).

13. See Kate Bowler, *Everything Happens for a Reason (and Other Lies I've Loved)* (New York: Random House, 2018). For Kate's wonderful podcast, see katebowler.com/everything-happens.

14. See Nicholas Wolterstorff, *Lament for a Son* (Grand Rapids: Eerdmans, 1987).

alone. Fundamentally then, any man can, under such circumstances, decide what shall become of him—mentally and spiritually."[15]

Etty Hillesum, facing death while imprisoned in the Westerbork Nazi transit camp in northern Holland, was somehow able to keep her focus on helping others. She wrote in her journal before being transferred to Auschwitz, where she was eventually murdered: "We should be willing to act as a balm for all wounds."[16]

I consider each of these women and men, living and dead, my mentors. Their lives have the ring of authenticity and exert a unique moral authority. Having deeply suffered, they remained faithful even in the midst of the most hellish circumstances imaginable. They have helped me put the pain and struggle of my own life into perspective. I don't mean that their heroism minimizes my own trials, but their stories help me "right-size" my struggles. Their faithfulness helps me tell myself a more hopeful story. In order to keep running our races, it sometimes helps to know that others have gone before us and experienced the worst that life has to offer yet found the strength to take another step.

These teachers are like those in Hebrews 11, the chapter we often call the "faith hall of fame." Like Abel, they still speak, even after they are dead (see v. 4). They lean over the railing of heaven, encouraging us to take one more step, get up one more time, keep searching for traces of grace and glimmers of hope, keep working and praying so that God's vision spoken through the prophet Amos will be realized: "But let justice roll on like a river, righteousness like a never-failing stream!" (Amos 5:24).

Digging a Deeper Well

Each of these faithful ones reminds me that we must dig our personal wells deep enough for there to be water to draw from

---

15. Viktor Frankl, *Man's Search for Meaning* (Boston: Beacon Press, 1959), 66.
16. Etty Hillesum, *Etty Hillesum: An Interrupted Life and Letters from Westerbork* (New York: Metropolis Books, 1996), 230–31.

during the driest times of life. More than twenty years ago, I started doing compassionate ministry projects in Africa when I began teaching for a month each summer at Africa Nazarene University in Nairobi, Kenya. I met and connected deeply with several of the students I taught, who went back to their home countries following graduation to become pastors and district superintendents. Several invited me to visit them and share ministry together. From these significant friendships, we eventually started a nonprofit organization, Compassion for Africa, that partners with Nazarene Compassionate Ministries in Ghana, Democratic Republic of the Congo, and Rwanda.[17]

Over the years we've learned a few things about digging wells. One of the most important things is to dig during the dry season, when the water table is at its lowest. If the well is deep enough to provide plenty of water during the driest times, then there will be enough water throughout the year. Recall Jesus's words about the wise man who "dug down deep" when he built his house on a solid foundation (Luke 6:48). We learned this lesson by trial and error, of course. Early on we dug a few wells when the rain was still falling, only to discover later, during the dry season, that the wells had dried up, disappointing and inconveniencing hundreds who had grown to count on the wells as reliable and safe sources of water. These wells were later re-dug during the dry season. These painful experiences taught me that resilience is an intentional process of digging a deeper well that can sustain us and those we love even during the driest times of our lives.

Resilience Is Like Building a House

Cultivating resilient character is also similar to building a house. It takes time and is deeply intentional. It cannot wait until we are in the eye of the storm. By then it's too late. We can build our

---

17. See www.compassionforafrica.org.

house on sand with the cheapest and most convenient materials possible; or we can build on a solid foundation with high-quality materials that will withstand the fiercest of storms. We cannot escape the storms of life, but with God's help and the companionship of others, we can nurture the strength of soul necessary to remain faithful in the midst of them.

In the Sermon on the Mount, Jesus says that wise people— often those who have lived a little and made some mistakes but have learned from those mistakes—have learned to build their lives on solid rock. Even when it rains, the streams rise, and the winds howl and beat their fists on the house, the house built on rock stands. Not so the foolish. For the foolish, anyplace will do. "This looks to me like as good a spot as any," they may say. But when the rain is incessant, the waters rise, and the winds rage, the house built on sand is swept away (see Matthew 7:24–27). Jesus's parable reminds me of the story "The Three Little Pigs." All three pigs build a house. Two foolishly build their houses out of inferior materials. They never pause to ask, "What about the Big Bad Wolf? Will my house protect me if he finds me?"[18] The story of our lives is that the Big Bad Wolf never fails to find us.

We're each building a life. We can be wise or foolish about the life we're building. Will the life we're building stand when the Big Bad Wolf comes knocking? What will happen to our house when the winds howl and the rains beat against it? Will it stand?

Scripture Is a Story of Resilience

From start to finish, the Bible is unashamed of telling story after story of how God's people grew weary, discouraged, distracted, and lost heart on the long journey of faithfulness. I find it life-giving to know we are not the first generation to face hard times. We are not the only ones who have ever wanted to give

18. John Ortberg talks about this topic as well in *Love Beyond Reason: Moving God's Love from Your Head to Your Heart* (Grand Rapids: Zondervan, 2001), 78.

up. If those who have gone before us can persevere, then perhaps so can you and I.

The story of God's people throughout history has largely been one of resilience in the face of tests and trials. Think of how the Israelites find the courage to resist slavery in Egypt; their ability to "sing the songs of the LORD while in a foreign land" during Babylonian captivity (Psalm 137:4); or the resilience of early Christians enduring persecution at the hands of the Roman Empire. The ultimate challenge to resilience for the first disciples was Jesus's crucifixion. Their hopes were crucified along with Jesus. The Roman Empire seemingly proved invincible. The two disciples on the road to Emmaus after the crucifixion reflect the despair of the first disciples, and often ours as well: "But we had hoped" (Luke 24:21a).

Early on Easter morning, the two Marys visit Jesus's tomb, where they meet an angel who tells them a story that is so good it *must* be true: Jesus is not dead but alive! Not able to fully grasp the angel's message, they run away from the tomb "afraid yet filled with joy" (Matthew 28:8). In the midst of their fear and budding excitement, they just so happen to bump into the resurrected Jesus. Daring to believe, the women clasp Jesus's feet and worship him. Filled with living hope, Jesus appoints the Marys to be the first preachers of the resurrection. They tell the male disciples that Jesus is not dead but alive! Word of God raising his Son from the dead quickly spreads—and it hasn't quit spreading for more than two thousand years. Our story as God's people has always been one of resilience in the face of death and despair. As difficult as it is to hope at times, God's people truly are "prisoners of hope" (Zechariah 9:12). What we are going through in our day is another chapter in God's ongoing story of faithful love.

Resilience is thus grounded in resurrection hope. Several years ago I came across this simple statement about hope that I have never forgotten: *Humans can live about forty days without food. Three days without water. Ten minutes without oxygen. But we cannot live for one second without hope.* Hopelessness is our greatest enemy. Hope energizes us. It's what gets us up and moving in the morning. Hope broadens the horizon from today to tomorrow and beyond. Hope is at the center of Christian faith. Hope is to the Christian what oxygen is to human life. No hope, no resilience. Writing out of his experience of hope in the midst of despair as a prisoner of war during World War II, Jürgen Moltmann speaks of Christian hope as

> the power of the resurrection from life's failures and defeats . . . the courage for living which hope quickens in us, so that we can get up again out of our failures, disappointments and defeats, and begin life afresh. No one is perfect, and few people succeed in achieving an unbroken continuity in their lives. Again and again we come up against limits and experience the failure of our plans for life. . . . Christian faith is faith in the resurrection, and resurrection is literally just that: rising up again. It gives us the strength to get up. . . . That is truly the revolutionary power of hope.[19]

Resurrection resilience is, as Moltmann so beautifully says, "rising up again." And, I would add, rising up again and again and again.

Uncertain times can prompt us to search for a better way forward. Crises can be a wake-up call or an opportunity for growth. Pain and disruption are often our best teachers if we're able to lean into them and listen. They can lead us to take inventory of our lives: *What are my priorities? What truly matters? Am I living up to the deepest values of my faith? How can I develop the strength of character to live a life of faith, hope, and love even in the midst of distressing times?* If we are to develop the character to withstand the setbacks and storms that threaten to overwhelm us, we will need as much life flowing *into* us as flows *out* of us.

---

19. Jürgen Moltmann, *In the End—the Beginning: The Life of Hope*, trans. Margaret Kohl (Minneapolis: Fortress Press, 2004), ix, xi.

The more life there is flowing into us, the greater our strength will be to bounce back, to have a fighting chance to survive both the expected and unexpected storms of life. Giving ourselves this fighting chance will require that we build into our lives certain practices that can help sustain us during dark times. Such practices—what can also be called habits—guide us and hold us fast when we don't know what else to do. Practices and habits of resilience lead to the development of character. Character is like the keel on a sailboat. If we are blown over, the keel helps us to spring back up, to remain buoyant. Character keeps us upright when otherwise we'd remain tipped over and vulnerable to the next wave.

This book is an exploration of the resources of Christian faith that can sustain us during times of trial and temptation. To be resilient requires something from us, as is the case for all the important things we commit ourselves to in life. So how do we harden, steel, strengthen, train, and prepare ourselves for the setbacks of life? There are indeed many practices that can strengthen our character and deepen our root system, and I will talk about many that have been helpful for me while following Christ, but the truth is, there are no easy, pain-free steps toward resilience. Resilience is often messy and unpredictable.

Anne Lamott adds a little humor to what can feel like an overwhelming process:

> It's funny: I always imagined when I was a kid that adults had some kind of inner toolbox, full of shiny tools: the saw of discernment, the hammer of wisdom, the sandpaper of patience. But then when I grew up I found that life handed you these rusty bent old tools—friendships, prayer, conscience, honesty—and said, *Do the best you can with these, they will have to do.* And mostly, against all odds, they're enough.[20]

---

20. Anne Lamott, *Traveling Mercies: Some Thoughts on Faith* (New York, Anchor Books, 2000), 103.

Humor nurtures both hope and resilience. Like John Stephen Akhwari, simply staying in the race, no matter how long it takes or how much we may hobble along the way, is what it means to be resilient. In the next chapter, we will look at the importance of Christlike self-love—learning to love ourselves as unconditionally as God does—for running our God-given race well.

FOR REFLECTION

- What practices currently help you remain resilient in the storms of life?
- What practices, relationships, or experiences are saving you these days?
- Who are the mentors (living or dead) who tutor you in faithfulness to Christ and remaining resilient and hopeful during trying times? If you don't have any, consider looking up the writings from some of the names mentioned earlier in this chapter as a starting point.
- How can you help others in your life to be more resilient?
- How deep have you dug your well? Take some time to consider whether it is deep enough to sustain you during difficult times.

THE BELOVED OF GOD

The Staying Power of Christlike Self-Love

RESILIENCE TIP

Resilient people learn to live confident and compassionate lives as the beloved of God, knowing that God's love for them and their love for God fuels their love for God's beloved world.

> *"I've realized why we're here," whispered the boy.*
> *"For cake?" asked the mole.*
> *"To love," said the boy.*
> *"And to be loved," said the horse.*
> —*Charlie Mackesy,* The Boy, the Mole, the Fox and the Horse

> *Love yourself. Then forget. Then, love the world.*
> —*Mary Oliver, "To Begin with, the Sweet Grass"*

> *We are loved and chosen as is, fearfully and wonderfully made, with love and awe, perfect and fragile.*
> —*Anne Lamott,* Almost Everything

> *Loving oneself is no easy matter . . . because it means loving all of oneself.*
> —*James Hillman*[1]

---

1. Cited in Jim Loehr and Tony Schwartz, *The Power of Full Engagement: Managing Energy, Not Time, Is the Key to High Performance and Personal Renewal* (New York: Simon and Schuster, 2003), 162.

Self-love, my liege, is not so vile a sin as self-neglecting.
—*William Shakespeare,* Henry V

The love of God is the sovereign remedy for all miseries.
—*John Wesley,* A Primitive Physic

We cannot accept love from another human being when we do not love ourselves, much less accept that God could possibly love us.
—*Brennan Manning,* Abba's Child

At first glance it may seem strange to include a chapter on self-love in a book about resilience. In my own efforts to remain resilient in the midst of the setbacks and storms of life, it is only remaining anchored in God's love for me and the love I have for myself that has enabled me to keep running my God-given race well. As the apostle Paul reminds us, love perseveres, hopes, and stands strong (see 1 Corinthians 13). Love is tender, but there's nothing stronger. The love of God keeps going and going and going. We may get knocked down, chewed up, and spit out by life (see 2 Corinthians 4:7–9), but the love of God always has the last word, and because of this, we have hope. So love is where we begin: God's love for each of us, for all humankind and for all creation, including all creatures. Each of us desperately yearns to know in the depths of our soul that we are loved for who we are. Period. No strings attached. Nothing to prove. Nothing to lose. Each of us needs to be regularly reminded of how deeply loved we are because we have a way of forgetting the things we need to remember and remembering the things we need to forget.

In the earliest days of being a pastor, I came up with a benediction that communicated the kind of community I believed God wanted our church to be. It echoes 1 John 4 and Jesus's words in John 13 but wasn't original to me. It went like this: "I love you. God loves you. Let's love one another." I pronounced this benediction—"blessing"—every Sunday at the close of our worship service for several years. As I grew in my theology of worship, I tried to change the benediction to something that quoted Scripture more directly. The people in my church were adamant that I keep the old one. So I went back to, "I love you. God loves you. Let's love one another."

I said this benediction to the same congregation every week for twenty-one years. It wasn't until I started reflecting on the power of sanctified self-love in cultivating resilience that I began to understand why the words were so important for my congregation to hear each week.[2] Clearly, we all need to know we're loved. Those of us who are married or have children hopefully hear and say, "I love you" several times a day. Others who live alone without close friendships or who find themselves in loveless relationships may rarely hear or say, "I love you."

The soul is desperately thirsty to receive the gift of belovedness. Love constitutes our very being. Love is who we are because God made us in the image of divine Love. In telling one another, "I love you," we communicate, *You are valued. You are beloved.* We are reminded of our true identity in Christ. Because we are the beloved of God, we are better able to persist through the setbacks of life, better able to shake off criticism because we know criticism often says more about the critic than it does about us. If we stumble, fall, or fail, we have assurance that our core identity is not made up of our mistakes but of our belovedness as children of God.

Anne Lamott tells of another pastor who understands how much his congregation needs to be reassured weekly that they are the beloved of God:

Every Sunday . . . he stands in front of everyone and tells them that they are beautiful, and God loves them exactly the way they

---

2. I use the terms "sanctified self-love" and "Christlike self-love" to distinguish a particularly Christian way of loving ourselves from the kind of self-love that is referenced in 2 Timothy 3:2, for example. The "lovers of themselves" spoken of in 2 Timothy could not be further from the kind of holy love Scripture teaches us to have for ourselves.

are, and they really don't have to worry because they have each other. But then by Tuesday they forget this, so on Sunday he goes back to their church and tells them that they are beautiful, and God loves them just the way they are, and they don't have to worry because they all have each other.[3]

For those of us who are pastors, one of the most significant things we do—but probably don't reflect on its importance nearly enough—is telling our congregation we love them. We do this with words but also by listening, sending notes, or giving hugs when appropriate. There were many senior adults in my church who were single and lived alone. I'm an affectionate person, so I started giving tentative hugs in my early days as a pastor, unsure how it would be received. Before long the seniors were the ones initiating the hugs. I wasn't taught in seminary the value of sharing love in these ways, but as I reflect on my ministry now, these were likely some of the most enduring and important things I did all week.

God's Love Is the Foundation and Purpose of Our Lives

God created us—and everyone who has ever existed—*in* love and *for* love. Like a potter, God lovingly scooped up a handful of soil, took a deep breath, and breathed life into Adam and Eve. From the very beginning there is a tenderness in the way God creates and remains with us. Because God knows our "inmost being" (Psalm 139:13), God knows better than anyone our potential and our fragility. God's love is intimate and deep, coursing through every cell in our body as well as upholding and inhabiting every atom in the universe.

We live in a God-soaked world where it is truly the love of God all the way down.[4] There is nothing deeper or more primordial

---

3. Anne Lamott, *Dusk. Night. Dawn: On Revival and Courage* (New York: Riverhead Books, 2021), 8.

4. See Richard Rohr, *The Universal Christ: How a Forgotten Reality Can Change Everything We See, Hope for, and Believe* (New York: Convergent, 2019).

than the love of God. God's love is everywhere, circulating in and through all things—and that includes you and me. Humanity has been created in the image of God, who is love itself. In response to such incredible love, what if we lived our lives as if God truly and unconditionally loves us? How would this change the way we view God, understand ourselves, love others, respond to injustices, or react to difficulty? How does the love of God deepen our resilience?

Dare to imagine that your very DNA is encoded with the love of God. You are truly loved at an atomic level. As much as we may be tempted at times—because of guilt or shame—to ignore, deny, or run away from God's love, we cannot escape it. The psalmist revels in God's persistent and pervasive presence: "If I go up to the heavens, you are there; if I make my bed in the depths, you are there" (139:8). The apostle Paul shares a similar message of God's anchoring love in his own life when he affirms that literally nothing—no circumstances, no mistakes, no shame—is ever "able to separate us from the love of God that is in Christ Jesus our Lord" (Romans 8:39). None of us can ever mess up our lives so badly that God's love does not remain with us. It's grace from beginning to end:

> The grace of God means something like: "Here is your life. You might never have been, but you are, because the party wouldn't have been complete without you. Here is the world. Beautiful and terrible things will happen. Don't be afraid. I am with you. Nothing can ever separate us. It's for you I created the universe. I love you." There's only one catch. Like any other gift, the gift of grace can be yours only if you'll reach out and take it.[5]

That we are created in the image of the loving God means we were created with the capacity to love and be loved. Loving ourselves is nothing less than imitating the love of the God who first

---

5. Frederick Buechner, *Wishful Thinking: Daily Readings in the ABCs of Faith* (New York: HarperOne, 2004), 139.

loved us. How could it be otherwise? When we help others love themselves as God loves them, we help to instill and restore self-worth, value, and dignity to all of God's beloved children. Henri Nouwen highlights the importance of accepting and living into the reality that we are indeed the beloved of God: "Self-rejection is the greatest enemy of the spiritual life because it contradicts the sacred voice that calls us the 'Beloved.' Being the Beloved constitutes the core truth of our existence."[6]

God loves us. Period. Without condition. It's a simple message that is difficult to embrace. The assurance that we are fully loved gives us the courage to come to God, even in the midst of the mess, muck, and mire of our lives. Can we dare to let God love us even in our worst moments? Our temptation is to withdraw from God when we feel unworthy or unforgiveable, but only Love can heal our deepest wounds.

The image that comes to mind when reflecting on our vulnerability before God is Jesus washing the disciples' feet. Can it be more clear than this that God is not repulsed by the mess of our lives but is willing to get dirty in drawing near to us? Jesus—fully human and fully God—takes the imperfect disciples' feet into his hands and washes the dirt, muck, and mire that accumulated by walking the dusty roads of Jerusalem. Perhaps there are even echoes here of God's intimacy in creating Adam and Eve from the soil of the garden of Eden. In this moment we see the curtains pulled back and the servant heart of God that has existed from all eternity revealed in Jesus's self-giving act of love. God's way with God's creation has always been as one who serves, gives, loves, and dares to call us friends (John 15:13–15).

The assurance that we are loved by God *no matter what* can get us through anything—setbacks, failures, devastating loss. As Paul

---

6. Henri J. M. Nouwen, *Life of the Beloved: Spiritual Living in a Secular World* (New York: The Crossroad Publishing Company, 1992), 28. Another writer who has helped me tremendously in the area of living into God's unconditional love is Brennan Manning. See his books *The Ragamuffin Gospel* and *Abba's Child*.

reminds us in 1 Corinthians 13, love never fails. Love perseveres. Love doesn't keep score. Love never gives up. Love believes the best of us. Love expressed as resurrection hope provides "the vital energy" we need to rise up again and again and again.[7]

Jesus, the Beloved of God

Jesus lived from this same foundation as the beloved of God. At the very beginning of Jesus's ministry, the Holy Spirit descended upon him like a dove as he was raised out of the waters of baptism in the Jordan River by John. God spoke words to him that sustained him throughout his ministry all the way to the cross: "You are my Son, the Beloved; with you I am well pleased" (Mark 1:11, NRSVUE). Jesus lived his whole life as the beloved one. People loved him. People hated him. People accepted him. People rejected him. People wanted to make him king. People crucified him. But in the midst of it all, he remained the beloved—the one on whom his Father's favor rested. Precisely because he was safe in his Father's love, he was free to fully love others. As Richard Rohr observes, "Only beloved people can pass on belovedness."[8]

Jesus is our example for discerning a rhythm of receiving and giving love. He did not consider his belovedness something to be used for his own advantage but freely offered it to all (see Philippians 2:5–11). Jesus understood himself to be a conduit of God's love in all the places he moved and to all the people he healed.[9] As fully God and fully human, even though his life was one of intense service to others, Jesus did not neglect his own need for rest, food, prayer, silence, and solitude in spite of endless demands on his time. Jesus is our model for our own capacity to be loved

---

7. See Jürgen Moltmann, *In the End—the Beginning: The Life of Hope*, trans. Margaret Kohl (Minneapolis: Fortress Press, 2004), xi, 32.

8. Richard Rohr, "God Is Always Choosing People," Center for Contemplation and Action, July 2021, https://cac.org/god-is-always-choosing-people-2021-07-02.

9. Norman Wirzba, *Agrarian Spirit: Cultivating Faith, Community, and the Land* (Notre Dame, IN: University of Notre Dame Press, 2022), 147.

by God, to love ourselves, and in turn to make our belovedness available to others. As we see in the life and ministry of Jesus, loving ourselves as God loves us does not stop with us. The love of God cannot be contained. It spills over. It always flows out to our neighbor—especially to the least, the last, and the marginalized among us. Henri Nouwen reminds us that embracing our own belovedness will "always leads to a deep desire to bless others."[10] Genuine, Christ-centered self-love will always lead us to share and invite others into life as the beloved.

The assurance of his belovedness held Jesus like an anchor for the storms that were brewing on his horizon. You may recall that, right after Jesus is baptized, the Spirit drives him into the wilderness for a prolonged time of trial and testing. He fasts there for forty days and is tempted by Satan and is in the company of wild animals. In Matthew's Gospel, we are told that, as soon as he returns from the wilderness, Jesus hears that John the Baptist (who just baptized him) has been thrown in jail. He then calls his disciples and hits the road, healing people and preaching about the kingdom of God. His Father's assurance of his belovedness and his solitude in the desert held him fast. Such assurance can hold us as well.

We may have never thought of it this way before, but one of the most important ways we fulfill God's purposes in the world is by loving ourselves. Loving ourselves as one in need of love, tenderness, and forgiveness is crucial if we are to flesh out God's love in the world. Those of us who are parents delight in our children. Is it possible that God loves us any less than earthly parents love their children? And don't those of us who are parents want our children to develop a healthy self-love where they learn to think neither too highly nor too lowly of themselves? When we truly love ourselves, we are doing nothing less than imitating the love of God, who first loved us. And we create hope that this weary, wounded world just might one day be healed.

10. Nouwen, *Life of the Beloved*, 67.

Struggling to Love Myself

It's one thing to know the importance of self-love but another to fully embrace it. For much of my childhood and adolescence, I hated myself. As a child, I was told by my family that I was "big-boned" and that "eventually" my height would catch up to my weight. As the cartoon character Garfield the cat once said, "I'm not overweight. I'm just under tall." Well, my height never caught up to my weight. The kids in my neighborhood and school didn't call me big-boned. They called me many, many other names, as you can imagine.

My mother, like many of her generation, told me to tell the bullies and myself, "Sticks and stones may break my bones, but words will never hurt me." I know she was trying to help, but the truth is, those words traumatized me. They caused me what we often refer to today as "moral trauma." The taunts just about obliterated my sense of self. Maybe you have experienced something similar.

Those names entered into my bloodstream like a cancer spreading through my body. Like too many others, my weight became part of a deeply diminished self-identity. I believed I was not only fat but also stupid and worthless. I experienced deep shame that stayed with me for decades from the merciless teasing about my weight. C. S. Lewis saw clearly the destructive force of shame: "I sometimes think that shame, mere awkward, senseless shame, does as much toward preventing good acts and straightforward happiness as any of our vices can do."[11]

In grade school I experienced daily the physical pain of rejection. I often got horrible stomachaches at school. At the time I thought it was because of the food I ate for breakfast. Now that I've studied stress and trauma for many years, I'm confident it wasn't what I ate for breakfast but the stress that ate at me while I was at school or playing with neighborhood kids. My body was

---

11. C. S. Lewis, *A Grief Observed* (San Francisco: HarperOne, 2015), 9.

constantly on high alert, ready for the next tease or taunt. I felt so awful about myself that I often cried myself to sleep. So many times I hurt so bad I wanted to die. Fortunately, I did not have the means to inflict lethal self-harm. I truly don't know what I would have done in my worst moments if I had access to such means.

It's Difficult to Love Ourselves

The most significant writer in my life journey—who has helped me slowly learn to love myself as God does—has been the Catholic priest and writer Henri Nouwen (1932–1996). Nouwen struggled with feelings of inferiority and the need to prove his worth to others even though he wrote dozens of books and held prestigious teaching positions at Yale, Harvard, and elsewhere. He was a restless soul who often sought to fill the void of lovelessness he felt even as he was praised by both Catholics and Protestants for his accomplishments. Unlike many of his day, Nouwen did not keep his struggles a secret. He wrote freely of his depression and discouragement in his many books and published journals. Nouwen's vulnerability has given me the courage to practice vulnerability in my own life. It's one of the greatest gifts of his legacy to me.

It's important to know something about Nouwen's life; otherwise, we may miss the poignancy of his words. He engaged in a lifelong, restless search to receive God's embrace as God's beloved. Knowing this deepens my respect for him because I recognize my own restless search in his descriptions. In the following quote from his published journal *The Road to Daybreak*, he consoles himself with words he imagines God speaking to him every day:

> I love you because you are beautiful, made in my own image, an expression of my most intimate love. Do not judge yourself. Do not condemn yourself. Do not reject yourself. Let my love touch the deepest, most hidden corners of your heart and reveal to you

your own beauty, a beauty that you have lost sight of, but which will become visible to you again in the light of my mercy. Come, come, let me wipe your tears, and let my mouth come close to your ear and say to you, "I love you, I love you, I love you."[12]

Can you imagine the difference it would make in the way we think about ourselves, treat ourselves, and interact with others if we truly imbibed this message in the depths of our souls? Perhaps as part of your devotional rhythm, you will want to print this passage on a card and put it in a place where you can receive this message several times throughout your day.

Love Your Neighbor as Yourself

Conventional wisdom has told many of us: *In order to love others more, you need to love yourself less.* Or, *Love God first, your neighbor next, and yourself last.* This view of love is a "zero-sum game, where if we give love in one place we [think we] need to take away from somewhere else."[13] Such an understanding of love flows from a theology of scarcity rather than one of abundance. With God there is always more than enough love for everyone—even our enemies.

Jesus clarifies the inextricable relationship of God, our neighbor, and ourselves in the Greatest Commandment (Matthew 22:37–40). Here Jesus provides three strands of Christian formation: love God; love your neighbor; love yourself. Love of neighbor and love of self are vitally interconnected for Jesus. They are two sides of the same coin. It's one love working in two directions at once. Notice Jesus's message here: love your

---

12. Nouwen, *Spiritual Journals: The Genesee Diary, Gracias!, The Road to Daybreak* (New York: Continuum, 1997), 403. If you are interested in reading more of Nouwen, I recommend *Spiritual Journals* because it contains three of his published journals in one volume.

13. Samuel Wells, *Be Not Afraid: Facing Fear with Faith* (Grand Rapids: Brazos Press, 2011), 191.

neighbor *as* yourself, not *instead* of yourself.[14] He is not saying that we *either* love our neighbor *or* love ourselves. And he is not saying we love our neighbor *more* than ourselves or *instead* of ourselves. It's love neighbor *and* love self at the same time. There is more than enough love for all of us. We love God, ourselves, our neighbors, and all creation simultaneously.

God's love is expansive, pouring into us and out of us at the same time. Jesus's message is that we can love God, love our neighbor, and love ourselves at the same time. Jesus is not asking us to choose. We can do all simultaneously. Think of parents' love for their children. Parents often wonder after the birth of their first child how they could possibly love another child as much as they love this one. Then comes the second child, and *voila*! Their love expands. Such is the abundant, overflowing nature of love, especially God's love.

Some will still want to know: whom do we love first, our neighbor or ourselves? The short answer is yes! It's both. It's like trying to decide whether the chicken or the egg came first. Look at what happens if we switch Jesus's words around and say, "Love yourself as your neighbor." As Sam Wells wisely puts it, "In other words, regard yourself as the first among all the neighbors God calls you to love. God's got a lot to be doing with the whole creation, but the wonderful thing is, God has chosen to start with you."[15] That's great news for all of us! We don't have to choose between loving ourselves and loving others. God loves all of us, the entire world, while also loving each of us as if we were the only one.

Saint Catherine of Siena puts our potential quandary into clear focus: "You are your chief neighbor."[16] Catherine wrote

14. See Carmen Renee Berry and Mark Lloyd Taylor, *Loving Yourself as Your Neighbor: A Recovery Guide for Christians Escaping Burnout and Codependency* (San Francisco: Harper & Row, 1990). Thank you to my friend and colleague Diane Leclerc for lending me this wonderful book.

15. Thank you to Nicholas Carpenter for first pointing out to me the sermon upon which the chapter in Wells's book is based. For a YouTube video of the original sermon, see https://www.youtube.com/watch?v=RlT4ELtaRWk. It will be twenty minutes well spent.

16. Catherine of Siena, *The Dialogue*, in *Classics of Western Spirituality* (Mahwah, NJ: Paulist Press, 1980), 33.

these words more than six hundred years ago. She only lived to be thirty-three years old, but she learned in her short life what takes many a lifetime to figure out: the Christian life is a journey of loving God and others, but it is also a journey of learning to love ourselves. Sam Wells puts it this way: "We're able to love others because of the way God loves us. And to accept that love, we have to learn to love ourselves."[17] As Catherine reminds us, the first neighbor God calls us to love is ourselves. Loving ourselves as our neighbor will likely go against the grain of what many of us have been taught. But yet the logic is simple: *if I do not know how to love myself, how can I possibly know how to truly love my neighbor?*

Too often we talk about loving our neighbor and caring for ourselves as if the two are disconnected. But sometimes we ourselves are the neighbor most in need of our love and tender care. As Sam Wells says again, "You love others best by loving yourself first. . . . The best way I can . . . teach you to love *yourself* is to love *myself* because being a Christian requires me to love myself as I love you."[18] Often the most loving thing we can do for our neighbor is lovingly care for ourselves. To love God and care for our neighbor well, we need to learn to care well for ourselves. It sounds simple, but it will be one of the most difficult things we ever do.

Golden-Rule Love

In both the Greatest Commandment and the Golden Rule, Jesus invites us to learn to love our neighbor by imagining how we like to be loved. In nine short words near the end of the Sermon on the Mount, Jesus summarizes the law and the prophets: "Treat others as you want them to treat you" (Matthew 7:12a, CEV). Golden-Rule love says, *I'm going to love you in the ways I like to be loved.*

---

17. Wells, *Be Not Afraid*, 192.
18. Wells, *Be Not Afraid*, 192, 193.

Golden-Rule love works like this: we reflect on our experience of being loved and imagine what that might look like in someone else's life. If our love language is strawberry rhubarb pie, for example, we may show love to others by the gift of strawberry rhubarb pie. Or, if we like flowers, we might give our neighbor flowers because it's what we would like someone to do for us if the roles were reversed. Here's a personal example: because I value clean water, education, and healthcare, I started the nonprofit organization Compassion for Africa more than twenty years ago to help those in rural areas of Ghana, Rwanda, and the Democratic Republic of Congo have access to these things. Compassion for others and working for Christlike justice is one of the main components of my love language.

What if we reverse the Golden Rule by treating ourselves the way we treat others? Sam Wells affirms that we know best how to love others by learning to love ourselves: "You love others best by loving yourself first."[19] This may come as a bit of a shock because most of us have an easier time treating others better than we treat ourselves. Ironically, it's often easier to be kind to others than to ourselves, especially when it comes to failure. Think, for example, how we might treat a friend who has failed: *God is merciful. God forgives us seventy times seven (see Matthew 18:22). Give yourself a break. Think of what was going on at the time. There were circumstances beyond your control. If it weren't for such-and-such, things would have worked out. This setback has nothing to do with your character. This is a one-time event. Yes, you made a mistake, but this is not who you are. It's not permanent. It's a temporary setback.* Fanny Howe expresses beautifully our desire to show ourselves the same love we demonstrate to others: "To have the height to view myself as I view others with lenience and love."[20]

Christlike self-care is self-compassion, treating ourselves with the kindness and mercy with which God treats us and we seek

---

19. Wells, *Be Not Afraid*, 192.
20. Fanny Howe, "But I Too Want to Be a Poet," *Joy: 100 Poems*, ed. Christian Wiman (New Haven, CT: Yale University Press, 2017), 125.

to treat others. If someone has always treated themselves with loathing or contempt, how can they ever truly love someone else with Christlike compassion and mercy? It will take a great deal of healing before that's possible. Think of how we often talk to ourselves when we make a mistake. We're sometimes tempted to view our mistakes as life-defining events from which we will never recover. In our self-talk, we are tempted to shame ourselves: *I'm a failure. What's wrong with me? I'll never amount to anything. I never do anything right. I might as well give up.* The truth is, if we talked to our friends the way many of us talk to ourselves, we would have few friends.

We can be incredibly harsh with ourselves when what we really need is gentle, merciful, compassionate conversation with ourselves. We don't improve or grow when we shame ourselves but only when we accept ourselves, warts and all, just as God does. As Carl Rogers famously said, "The curious paradox is that when I accept myself just as I am, then I can change." This opportunity for transformation through accepting love is exactly what God offers us in Christ. God loves us as much in our failures as in our successes. Anne Lamott challenges those of us who are tempted to chronically critique ourselves: "Learn to be more compassionate company, as if you were somebody you are fond of and wish to encourage."[21]

Reprogramming Old Software

No matter how attractive a loving relationship with ourselves may sound, many of us have old software running in our minds, telling us that loving ourselves is at worst sinful and at best misleading. It will be difficult to reprogram that mental software, but it can be done with consistent intentionality. Here is a slice of someone's journey of learning not only to like herself but truly love herself:

---

21. Anne Lamott, *Bird by Bird: Some Instructions on Writing and Life* (New York: Pantheon Books, 1994), 31.

Mary grew up thinking it was selfish to love herself. She learned an acronym in Sunday school that still guided her prayers and interactions with others almost forty years later. The acronym was JOY: Jesus first, Others second, Yourself last.

She said, "I was always taught that putting my needs before others was selfish and sinful. I learned early that my concerns were less important than those of others. Even today I still feel guilty talking about my own needs when the needs of others seem so much greater than my own. It's taken me a long time, but because of loving pastors and Christian friends, I'm slowly learning that God wants me to love myself. I am God's beloved daughter, lovingly created in God's image. I don't know why it took so long, but it's finally dawning on me that it is precisely because I love God, my family, and others that I must also love myself. If I truly love those who love me, it only makes sense that I will tend to my own needs for rest, regular exercise, and healthier eating habits. I'm also reminded that Jesus said that we are to treat others the way we want to be treated. If I don't know how to love myself, how can I possibly know how to love others?"

Like Mary, you may have been taught the JOY acronym as a guide to the Christian life. When Jesus gave the Greatest Commandment, he was not naming a hierarchical order. As we have already seen, it's not that we love Jesus *at the expense of* others or ourselves but that we love Jesus *so that* we can fully love others and ourselves—at the same time.

Balancing Our Needs with the Needs of Others

In 2001, I started traveling in the summers to teach and do various compassionate ministry projects. After my second month-long trip to Kenya to teach at Africa Nazarene University in Nairobi, I returned home concerned about what my annual trips might be communicating to my two children, who were ten and seven at the time. They both loved the wood and soapstone carvings I brought home with me. They enjoyed hearing about the new friends I made from other countries whose lives were so different from our own. They were enthralled with the pictures of lions, elephants, giraffes, and other animals I took while on safari. Yet I was in a quandary.

I believed God wanted me to continue traveling, teaching, and resourcing local leaders in Africa. My wife, Shelly, and the congregation I was pastoring at the time wholeheartedly supported me. But I didn't want Jimmie and Annie to feel that I loved them less than the children in Africa I served. I had seen and heard of too many pastors who neglected their own families in their quest to "save the world." I didn't want to save the world yet lose my family. I worried and fretted for several weeks before it finally dawned on me simply to ask them how they felt about my trips. Jimmie had no problem with my going as long as I kept bringing him back souvenirs.

Annie responded, swinging her legs back and forth, "Daddy, we need you, but they need you too."

I will never forget that moment. Her words were an epiphany for me. Hers was the voice of God to me. And it was a blessing to so many in Africa. Annie taught me that loving ourselves and loving others is not a zero-sum game where there are only winners and losers. In God's economy, there is enough for all. Caring for our personal and family needs does not need to be in competition with or opposition to the needs of others. Because Annie felt secure in my love for her, she was free to share me with others. She knew there was enough love for her *and* for our friends in Africa. Even at seven, Annie had already discovered the wisdom behind Mary Wollstonecraft's words: "Genuine duties support each other."[22] What this quote says to me is this: *Your needs are not opposed to mine. Your health is not in opposition to mine.* The needs of others, near or far away, are not opposed to mine. Like

---

22. Mary Wollstonecraft, *A Vindication of the Rights of Woman*, (Oxford: Oxford University Press, 2009), 189. Thank you to Julie Straight for introducing me to Wollstonecraft.

a few dried fish and loaves of bread, there is always enough of God's love to go around.

Since Annie's and my conversation more than twenty years ago, I have traveled to Africa more than a dozen times for anywhere from three to eight weeks at a time. Rather than my absences detracting from our family, my trips have enhanced our family life. When Annie was a senior in high school, she started baking cupcakes to raise money for a medical clinic in Ghana. I will tell the rest of that story in a later chapter. In fact, my travel, ministry, and lifelong friendships in Africa have sustained my family and me through some very difficult times. In light of the purpose of this book, I can say without hesitation that these connections have made our family more resilient in the face of setback and loss.

When Paul says in Philippians, "Let each of you look not to your own interests but to the interests of others" (2:4, NRSVUE), he is not saying that our own interests are unimportant. He is simply saying that our interests should not be so consuming that we neglect the legitimate needs of others.[23] There is indeed an appropriate love of the self in Scripture that can be said to be Christlike in its fundamental orientation. I call this "sanctified self-love." Christlike self-love looks *not only* to its own interests *but also* to the interests of others. Paul acknowledges that it's right and proper to look after our own interests. His point is that our love must not stop with our own legitimate concerns but always also extend to others. Paul goes on to express that our service to others is a reflection of the service of Christ, "who, being in very nature God, did not consider equality with God something to be used to his own advantage; rather, he made himself nothing by taking the very nature of a servant" (vv. 6–7a).

Out of the abundant and overflowing life of the Trinity, Jesus was able to freely offer himself in service to the world. As we think

---

23. See Dean Flemming, *Philippians: A Commentary in the Wesleyan Tradition*, New Beacon Bible Commentary (Kansas City, MO: Beacon Hill Press of Kansas City, 2009), 104–105.

about our own service to others, we will do well to recall that, "Out of the fullness of love, not out of the emptiness of need, God made and redeemed the world through Jesus Christ."[24] Only in the context of the fullness of Trinitarian life and the abundance of Jesus's own life can loving ourselves as a way of loving our neighbors make sense. There is, indeed, more than enough of God's grace for you, me, our neighbors, and all creatures and creation.

Scripture's theological logic for Christian self-love is simple: since we are called to imitate God, and God loves the entire world, we are to love ourselves as an expression of God's love for the world.[25] Since we are called to be loving, kind, compassionate, gentle, and generous toward others, why would we withhold these basic considerations from ourselves? A former student of mine, Nicholas Carpenter, wisely observed, "Christians must be people who give themselves the love they proclaim toward others. If Christians do not love themselves as they love others, it is as though they refuse to take the healing medicine they give to others who are just as sick. Christians must be willing to receive love and grace, from both God and others, if they are to live the fullest life of love available to them."[26]

It may be that you've been taught that self-love, like sin, needs to be eradicated from your life. We've all known people who are self-absorbed, unconcerned, and disconnected from the needs of others. They exist. There's no denying it. But true biblical, Christ-centered self-love has nothing in common with such narcissism.

Self-Love and Self-Denial

Jesus commands the disciples to deny themselves and take up their cross daily (Matthew 16:24; Mark 8:34; Luke 9:23).

---

24. Berry and Taylor, *Loving Yourself as Your Neighbor*, 130.

25. See Thomas Jay Oord, *The Nature of Love: A Theology* (Chalice Press, 2000), 13, 28.

26. Nicholas Carpenter, forum post, in Northwest Nazarene University's Graduate Theological Online Program, October 2015. Thank you to Nick for his permission to include his words here.

Self-denial and cross-bearing do not mean we are to reject or neglect the health of our God-created selves, however. The biblical understanding of self-denial is not to hate ourselves by being self-neglecting or self-rejecting. The kind of self-denial Jesus is referencing here has nothing to do with rejecting the self that loves family, appreciates sunsets, sings, laughs, or enjoys eating good food. Instead, it has to do with the reordering of our commitments so that Christ is the Lord of our lives.[27] Christian self-denial is saying yes to Christ and no to anything or anyone that stands in the way of loving God and neighbor. We can say yes to Christ while also saying yes to many of the other wonderful experiences of life God has set before us.

Christian self-denial is also never to be equated with neglecting our emotional or physical needs. Christian self-denial has nothing to do with self-loathing or self-criticism. Mark Galli makes the point crystal clear when he observes, "In case you hadn't heard, self-loathing is not a fruit of the Spirit."[28] Taking up our cross is also not the same as self-neglect. Jesus, for example, did not neglect his needs for rest, food, prayer, silence, and solitude. Jesus even spent extended times away from those he was sent to love in order to tend to his own needs and be alone with his heavenly Father. God does not intend for us to destroy ourselves through lack of healthy self-care.

If there is indeed a healthy, Christ-centered self-love, what might the kind of selfishness that is truly sinful look like? Certainly the kind of selfishness that is so wrapped up in itself it refuses to help the poor is sinful (see Deuteronomy 15:9). Self-interest that never looks out for the interests of others is clearly not the kind of self-love we're talking about either (see Philippians 2:3–4). There is also the kind of selfishness that fails to feed the hungry,

---

27. Archibald D. Hart, *Me, Myself, & I: How Far Should We Go in Our Search for Self-Fulfillment?* (Ann Arbor, MI: Servant Publications, 1992), 57.

28. Mark Galli, "Asking the Right Question, *Christianity Today*, April 2010, https://www.christianitytoday.com/ct/2010/aprilweb-only/23-51.0.html.

provide water to the thirsty, welcome the immigrant, clothe the naked, or visit the sick and imprisoned (see Matthew 25:31–46). Each of these unloving responses to our neighbors is sinful and not representative of the kind of abundant life to which God calls us for the sake of others. The kind of life orientation that ignores the needs of the vulnerable around us clearly misses the mark of God's loving intentions.

It really is possible to love ourselves while serving the needs of others. Our needs and the needs of others may be in tension with each other at times, but they are not fundamentally opposed even when it is difficult to discern the boundaries. This is not to say there will never be times when we should put the needs of others above our own, such as in cases of illness, accidents, or genuine emergencies. But in order to sustain lasting, vibrant health so that we are best able to respond well to the needs around us, we need to develop a sustainable and healthy rhythm that honors the needs of our own souls.

So how do we recognize those who pervert true, Christ-centered self-love? Jesus said it's easy: "You will know them by their fruits" (Matthew 7:16, NRSVUE). Distortion of the love God intends for us to have toward others and ourselves through self-addiction and self-idolatry is ugly. Second Timothy tells us that such "lovers of themselves" are those who are "self-absorbed, money-hungry, self-promoting, stuck-up, profane, contemptuous of parents, crude, coarse, dog-eat-dog, unbending, slanderers, impulsively wild, savage, cynical, treacherous, ruthless, bloated windbags, addicted to lust, and allergic to God" (3:2–4, MSG).

It's impossible to confuse such a self-absorbed, turned-in-upon-itself life with the expansive life of someone who is filled with the fruit of the Spirit of love that Paul describes in 1 Corinthians 13: "Love is patient, love is kind. It does not envy, it does not boast, it is not proud. It does not dishonor others, it is not self-seeking, it is not easily angered, it keeps no record of wrongs. Love does not delight in evil but rejoices with the truth. It always protects, always trusts, always hopes, always perseveres. Love never fails" (vv. 4–8a).

Those We Assume Love Themselves Too Much . . .

Many of the people we assume love themselves too much actually love themselves too little. Arrogance, for example, is most often an expression of insecurity rather than too much self-love. Often we misattribute arrogance as pride when instead it usually means there is too little self-love or a distorted sense of self-love at work. Truly selfish people are cut off from God's love or are so wounded by life's circumstances or by addiction that they can be a black hole of demands and expectations.

Sam Wells helps us imagine what a person who loves themselves too little may be thinking: "No one's looking out for me, so I'd better take as much as I can, while I can, so I have plenty for when things turn bad." For this reason, as Wells goes on to say, "Selfishness isn't a sign of too much self-love: it's quite the opposite. It's a sign of profound insecurity."[29] Christians who are secure in God's unconditional love do not need to grasp for more love for ourselves at the expense of loving others. Because of God's abundant generosity, we can rest assured that there will always be enough love to go around.

Spoon Theory

Spoon theory is a metaphor that was developed in 2003 by Christine Miserandino to describe life with chronic illness. The theory goes that each day people have a certain, limited number of spoons that represent our energy and ability to get that day's tasks done. Those with chronic illness or pain have to ration their daily spoon supply carefully because their spoons disappear

---

29. Wells, *Be Not Afraid*, 191.

faster, even while performing tasks that may seem basic to those without chronic pain or illness. For those who do experience chronic illness or pain, it is important to set clear boundaries as well as express clearly to others their limitations. Without clear communication, it's easy for others to misinterpret someone's lack of energy as withdrawal or a lack of love. And without clear boundaries, it's easy for those with chronic conditions to overdo it and spend more spoons than they actually have, thus borrowing from tomorrow's supply.[30]

Rationing physical and emotional energy is difficult for many reasons, especially since chronic pain or illness can vary greatly from one day to the next. There may be more or less to give, depending on the day. Those who live with such conditions may find it helpful to communicate spoon theory clearly with their loved ones so their loved ones can be present in appropriate ways. And those who love someone living with chronic pain may need to help their loved ones learn to love themselves. One of the ways this can be done is to regularly ask what they need on a given day and to be kind, gentle, and loving no matter how they may be feeling.

Loving Ourselves Is a Lifetime Project

If you find it difficult to care for yourself as an expression of God's love for you, I encourage you to start investing in and cultivating your own health as an act of love for those who love and need you most. A theology of health affirms that self-care is not selfish but gives us greater energy to love God and our neighbors wholeheartedly. Healthy people love. Healthy people are generous. Healthy people serve. Healthy people are physically strong, mentally alert, and emotionally resilient. Healthy

---

30. The Cleveland Clinic published an excellent article on spoon theory: "What Is the Spoon Theory Metaphor for Chronic Illness?" November 2021, https://health.clevelandclinic.org/spoon-theory-chronic-illness.

people are more loving spouses, patient parents, effective at work, and involved in service to others. Soul care is neighborly love extended toward ourselves, others, and all creation. We nourish ourselves so that all can flourish. The well-being of the world starts with our personal health that finds its source in God's own overflowing love. Sam Wells summarizes well the message of this chapter:

> This is the work of self-love: to let yourself be loved by Jesus, and to be so energized and transformed by that love that you love yourself as the first among all the countless neighbors God calls you to love. To learn to be their friend, you practice by being your own friend. You don't resent those neighbors because they're not taking away anything that belongs to you. You've already been looked after because, after being loved by Jesus, there's nothing more to want. By contrast, if you're looking everywhere to bolster your self-regard, I've got bad news for you: it will never be enough. It will be like pouring water into a jug with a leak at the bottom. Of course that's exhausting. In that economy, looking after yourself is bound to take away from looking after others.[31]

"I Want a Blessing"

One of the most transforming stories I have ever read about the power of blessing comes from Henri Nouwen's book *Life of the Beloved.* This story has shaped how I think about myself as the beloved of God and how I treat others as the beloved of God. Nouwen tells of a life-changing experience he had at the L'Arche community in Toronto where he was a chaplain.[32] *L'Arche* means "the ark" in French. L'Arche communities are formed throughout the world to be an ark of safety for those with mental and physical disability. L'Arche communities seek to provide a caring home environment while also offering spiritual hope to the residents

---

31. Wells, *Be Not Afraid*, 192.
32. I have paraphrased this story from Nouwen, *Life of the Beloved*, 57–59.

and their families. As of October 2022, there are 160 L'Arche communities in 38 countries.[33]

In his role as chaplain, Nouwen was leading a prayer service when Janet, a L'Arche community resident, unexpectedly came up in the middle of the service and asked, "Henri, can you give me a blessing?"

He responded, "Certainly, Janet," and began to make the sign of the cross on her forehead.

She interrupted him, protesting strongly, "Oh no, Father, that doesn't work. I want a real blessing!"

Henri wasn't sure exactly what she meant, so he asked her, "What do you mean by a real blessing, Janet?"

She didn't answer him but looked at him like he should know what she was talking about, since he was a priest after all.

Nouwen announced to the group of about thirty gathered for the service, "Janet has asked for a special blessing."

He still wasn't exactly sure what kind of blessing she wanted, but Janet didn't leave any doubt. As soon as he announced to the group that Janet wanted a special blessing, she spontaneously threw her arms around him and put her head on his chest.

He embraced her and said, "Janet, I want you to know that you are God's beloved daughter. You are precious in God's eyes. Your beautiful smile, your kindness to the people in your house, and all the good things you do show us what a beautiful human being you are. I know you feel a little low these days and that there is some sadness in your heart, but I want you to remember who you are: a very special person, deeply loved by God and all the people who are here with you."

Janet's face brightened as she received the love behind the words and the embrace.

As soon as Janet returned to her seat, Jane, another member of the community, raised her hand and said, "I want a blessing too!"

---

33. For an overview of the mission of L'Arche communities, see https://www.larche.org/about-larche/.

Before Nouwen knew it, she too had thrown her arms around him and laid her face against his chest. He blessed her as well.

Several more from the community expressed their desire to be blessed. One of the most touching moments that Nouwen relates is when a twenty-four-year-old assistant raised his hand and asked, "And what about me?"

Nouwen responded, "Sure, John, it is so good that you are here. You are God's beloved son. Your presence is a joy for all of us. When things are hard and life is burdensome, always remember that you are loved with an everlasting love."

John looked at Nouwen with tears in his eyes and simply said, "Thank you, thank you very much."

If we truly believe this—that we are the chosen, blessed, beloved children of God—then we will be truly free to care for others in Jesus's name. As one who is blessed by God, I can be a blessing to others in Jesus's name. Nouwen speaks of how the rhythm of blessedness makes possible the blessing of others: "The blessings that we give to each other are expressions of the blessing that rests on us from all eternity. It is the deepest affirmation of our true self. It is not enough to be chosen. We also need an ongoing blessing that allows us to hear in an ever-new way that we belong to a loving God who will never leave us alone but will remind us always that we are guided by love in every step of our lives."[34]

This story has sustained me through tough times for many years now. Perhaps you are going through a difficult stretch of life and need to be reminded that you're God's beloved, no matter your current or past circumstances or choices. There's no need to rehearse the depth or breadth of your pain. This moment you can receive the love of God that is always turned to its highest setting. Just like Nouwen with his L'Arche congregation, you can receive God's blessing: *you are indeed the beloved of God.* As difficult as it may be to embrace such unconditional love, you

---

34. Nouwen, *Life of the Beloved*, 59.

truly are the beloved of God upon whom God's love rests in the midst of failure, disappointment, setbacks, pain, illness, or broken relationships. You are loved. You are beloved exactly where you are, in the midst of whatever you're going through, because God is with you. God loves you as much on your good days as on your bad days. God has plans for God's people, but God also has plans for you.

The Transforming Power of Living as the Beloved of God

Our image of God creates us.[35] When we love ourselves as God loves us, we become more resilient, more faithful, more loving, more kind, more healthy, more courageous, and we enjoy more meaningful relationships. When we rest confidently in knowing ourselves as the beloved of God, we discover the power to resist temptations to despair, self-loathing, and hopelessness. Learning to love ourselves unconditionally as God does is an ongoing and absolutely necessary journey if we are to run our God-given race well.

More than anything else in my Christian life, living as the beloved of God has transformed me into who I am today. When I am tempted to compare myself with others, feel sorry for myself, or compelled to compete for accomplishments or acknowledgment, I come back to these words: *Joe, you are my beloved son with whom I am well pleased. I love you, period. No conditions. No strings attached. You cannot earn it or lose it. It is a gift. It is the deepest truth about you.*

Not only am I God's beloved, but I am also my wife's beloved. And my children's beloved. And my mother's beloved. They all love me as if they didn't have any better sense. This simple reality has changed me and healed me of many childhood traumas.

---

35. Richard Rohr, "God Is Good," Center for Action and Contemplation, September 2021, https://cac.org/god-is-good-2021-09-12/?&utm_source=twitter&utm_medium=social&utm_campaign=dm&utm_term=organic.

I trust their love for me. I live in and from its radiance. I don't have to question, doubt, demand, or be jealous of their love. There is more than enough love to go around. I simply rest in their love for me.

When you live in the moment-by-moment awareness that you are God's beloved child, your life will also be transformed. God's unconditional love, revealed in Jesus Christ, is the basis for all holy living because, when we sense that we are truly loved as much on our good days as on our bad days, we are free to "take hold of the life that is truly life" (1 Timothy 6:19). We will not worry so much about failing, or obsess over what others think about us, or be driven to achieve and accomplish in order to prove our worth. Because a holy, Christlike life rests securely in the love of God, such a life has nothing to prove and nothing to lose. As the beloved of God, we are able to truly and freely love ourselves, our neighbors, and all creatures and creation in Jesus's name. Out of God's overflowing generosity, there is always more than enough to go around.

As God's beloved, I encourage you to love yourself as if your life and the lives of others depend on it—because they do. Loving ourselves, like all means of grace, takes practice. Loving ourselves as God loves us will be one of the hardest things we will ever do. And we will need to stay at it every day. Loving ourselves as God does is a lifetime project. Living as the beloved of God will keep us resilient and help us grow in Christlike holiness. The security of living in the midst of God's love is a shock absorber against the bumps and bruises of everyday life. It insulates against the setbacks that come our way.

The great realization here is this: not only are you and I the beloved of God, but so is everyone else! As we grow in the implications of self-love, for the kind of love with which we are called to treat others, we will discover that there is enough of God's love to extend to everyone, even our enemies. And to the relatives we don't like. And to inconsiderate neighbors. And to those who cut us off in traffic. And to those who perpetuate injustice. There is no room for fear, anger, or exclusion in a heart taken up with the love of God we see revealed fully in Jesus. There is no scarcity of love in God. There is enough for me. There is enough for you. There is enough for our enemies and those we don't like very much. This kind of love will truly transform the world in Jesus's name.

FOR REFLECTION

- Who in your life has helped you recognize your true value? Consider reaching out and letting them know how much their love means to you.
- Why do you think many Christians feel uncomfortable loving themselves?
- What is the relationship between self-love and growing in Christlike holiness?
- What would developing an appropriate rhythm of self-love with service to others look like in your life? How do you balance your personal needs with the needs of others?
- What are your biggest obstacles—whether personal or theological—to loving yourself as your neighbor?
- How might caring better for yourself benefit those you love and serve? What specific steps can you begin to take toward loving yourself as your neighbor?
- Why is cultivating an authentic, Christ-centered self-love especially important for those with chronic illness, chronic pain, or disability?
- Tomorrow morning before you begin your day, take five to ten minutes to reflect on the following and say to yourself: *I am God's beloved child. God's love is in me and with me. God loves me, period. God loves me as much on my good days as on my bad days.*
- How do you think doing this might change the way you view yourself or the way you treat others?

2

TEARS IN A BOTTLE

Nurturing Resilience through Prayer

RESILIENCE TIP

Resilient people learn to regularly nurture their relationship with God through various forms of prayer.

> *What happens to all [my] prayers when not only are they not "answered," but things get far worse than anyone ever anticipated? What about prayer? We do not know. We will not know in this life. Some prayers are magnificently answered. More than once this has been the case in my own life, glorious miracles of prayer. . . . Surely the prayers have sustained me, are sustaining me. Perhaps there will be unexpected answers to these prayers, answers I may not even be aware of for years. But [my prayers] are not wasted. They are not lost. I do not know where they have gone, but I believe God holds them, hand outstretched to receive them like precious pearls.*
>
> —*Madeleine L'Engle,*
> Two-Part Invention: The Story of a Marriage

> *Prayer is a small fire lit to keep cold hands warm. Prayer is a practice that flourishes both with faith and doubt. Prayer is asking and prayer is sitting. Prayer is the breath. Prayer is not an answer, always, because not all questions can be answered.*
>
> —*Pádraig Ó Tuama,*
> Daily Prayer with the Corrymeela Community

> *Be joyful in hope, patient in affliction, faithful in prayer.*
> —*Romans 12:12*

To be people of resilience, there needs to be as much life flowing into us as flows out of us. Life *flows* out of us as we give of ourselves to others. Life *leaks* out of us through the stresses of everyday life. The daily paper cuts of life exact a toll. The needs around us often feel endless. And the results of our efforts can seem few and far between, insignificant and inconsistent. Then there are setbacks and even failures. The storms of life come upon us unexpectedly. We need God's Spirit to pour into our exhausted lives a constant, life-giving stream of "strength for today and bright hope for tomorrow."[1] One of the most important ways we draw upon God's strength for our weariness is through prayer.

Ever since I became a Christian as a high school senior, I've learned many important things about prayer. While I have a lot of practice in prayer, I've also failed and struggled with prayer. I've asked many questions along the way: *How do I pray? What do I pray? When do I pray? What about the prayers I pray for myself and others? What about unanswered prayer? What counts as prayer?* Because of my need to understand God more and pray better, I've read many books about prayer. I've taught others about prayer. I've learned about prayer from spiritual directors, and I've learned about prayer through my daily practice. The most important thing I've learned over the years is that prayer is primarily about showing up. Roberta Bondi wisely counsels: "Regularity is more sustaining in prayer than intensity or length."[2]

John Wesley referred to prayer as a means of grace.[3] Prayer and other means of grace are the ways we cooperate with the Holy Spirit's transforming work in us. Practicing means of grace puts us in a place to receive the grace of God. Means of grace are those habits, experiences, and relationships that help us steward

---

1. Thomas O. Chisholm (words) and William M. Runyan (music), "Great Is Thy Faithfulness," *Sing to the Lord: Hymnal* (Kansas City, MO: Lillenas Publishing Company, 1993), #44.

2. Roberta C. Bondi, "Paradox of Prayer," *Weavings* (March/April 1989), 9.

3. Wesley, "Sermon 16: The Means of Grace," *The Bicentennial Edition of the Works of John Wesley,* ed. Frank Baker (Nashville: Abingdon, 1984ff.), 1:376–97.

the Holy Spirit's transforming work in us so that we grow in the love of God for the sake of others. The primary means of grace for Wesley were worship, prayer, reading Scripture, and Communion, but he also included visiting the poor and the sick and extending God's justice to the vulnerable. More broadly understood, the means of grace can be anything that shapes us into the image of Christ for the sake of others.

The Rhythm of Our Prayers

Anne Lamott writes about three primal rhythms of prayer in her book *Help, Thanks, Wow: The Three Essential Prayers*. It's hard to think of a type of prayer that doesn't fit into one of these categories.

God, I need your help in finding a job.

God, my friends in Ghana without clean water need your help. I need your wisdom to know how I can best help them.

Loving God, there is way too much injustice and pain in the world. We desperately need your help!

Oh, what a wonderfully sweet peach I'm eating. Thank you, God!

Loving God, I'm so grateful for my family and friends.

God, the beauty on this walk is breathtaking. Wow! Wow! Wow!

There is a rhythm to our prayers.

We pray when we are hurting.

We pray when we are grateful.

We pray when we are afraid.

We pray when our feet slip.

We pray when we're broken-hearted.

We pray when we're anxious.

We pray when we're sinking into doubt.

We pray when we're in love.

We try to pray when we're in the clutches of depression but may only be able to groan and whimper (see Romans 8:26).

We pray for courage in the face of obstacles.

We pray for strength to step over our fear and do the next right thing even though the way ahead is unclear.

We pray for an infilling of love for those we don't like very much.

We pray for our enemies.

We pray to forgive those who have hurt us, knowing it takes a long, long time to heal a deep wound.

We pray for God's will to be done on earth as it is in heaven because, too often in this life, we see injustice with the upper hand.

We pray at all times and in many different ways, depending on the season of life in which we find ourselves.

For What Do We Pray?

We pray for whoever and whatever comes to mind. Just as in any healthy relationship, we can talk to God about anything. Whatever comes to mind is fair game to bring to God. We can speak words, or we can carry on a silent conversation with God. We can stand, sit, kneel, or walk. We can even pray while driving—but be sure to keep your eyes open!

We pray for ourselves. We pray to become more like Christ and to exhibit more clearly the fruit of the Spirit in our lives: "love, joy, peace, patience, kindness, generosity, faithfulness, gentleness, and self-control" (Galatians 5:22–23, NRSVUE). We pray for help when we don't know what to do. We pray for strength when we can't take another step. We pray for wisdom when we are in over our heads. We pray for the strength to remain steady "in season and out of season" (2 Timothy 4:2).

We pray for others, both near and far away. As we become more resilient, faithful, and courageous in our relationship with Christ, we can extend these qualities toward others. As Father James Martin says, "Praying for yourself all the time is like talking to yourself all the time. It not only demonstrates your selfishness, but also increases it. Others need your prayers as well."[4]

Perhaps somewhat surprisingly, we may discover that the answer to our prayers for others is often ourselves! If someone expresses a need to us, it's an act of love to let them know we'll be praying for them. If we tell someone we'll pray for them, then we need to be sure we actually pray for them—and then follow up with them. Sometimes I put a prayer request on a sticky note and post it on my computer screen where I'm sure to see it. Or I put the prayer request in my digital calendar to remind myself to pray or check up with the person after a certain amount of time has passed. Or we can express love the old-fashioned way by writing a note and putting it in the mail.

Prayer is also needed for widespread and deeply embedded issues. We pray for those experiencing poverty, homelessness, disability, mental illness. I have found that it's less difficult to pray for such weighty issues as a congregation or small group. Christian community strengthens our resilience in prayer, helping us be more courageous in our communal prayers than we are on our own.[5] The beginning of the Lord's Prayer reminds us that we never pray alone but with Christians around the world when say, "*Our* Father." Praying in solidarity with others provokes deeper faith and persistence.

Prayer Is Rooted in the Unconditional Love of God

Prayer, like other resilience-cultivating practices, is rooted in the unconditional love of God. This means it is love all the way down. The love of God inhabits and surrounds us. It's the air we breathe. It's in the blood that courses through our veins. Every

---

4. James Martin, SJ, *Learning to Pray: A Guide for Everyone* (San Francisco: HarperOne, 2021), 104.

5. For those who are pastors, an important book on prayer is David Busic's *The Praying Pastor* (Kansas City, MO: The Foundry Publishing, 2022).

time our heart beats we are reminded that God is with us and within us.

Jesus is our *Emmanuel*, God with us. In the incarnation not only did God become flesh, but God also invites us to see that we live in "a Christ-soaked world."[6] The incarnation radicalizes (in the sense of getting us to the root of things) how we understand the presence and love of God in humans and in all that God has created. This understanding has life-altering implications for resilient prayer. When we affirm that God is not only with us but also within us, we can never be truly alone. We may feel alone, abandoned even. But the theological truth is that, just as God fills the entire world, so also does God's Spirit dwell in every part of us, including our physical bodies.

Reflecting on God's radical nearness fills me with hope when I'm tempted to despair. It empowers me to keep working for justice and the renewal of all things in Christ, even when it seems that the powers and principalities of this world have the upper hand (see Ephesians 6:12). It keeps me praying in trying times. When we pray, we do not pray to a God who once upon a time created the world, wound it up like a clock, and watches from a distance as we are left to our own devices. In prayer we are constantly upheld by the ever-present love of God.

Because of this radical theology of God's nearness to us in Christ, we do not lose heart. For this reason the apostle Paul encourages the Galatians to remain faithful even when there are no visible signs of a harvest: "So let's not allow ourselves to get fatigued doing good. At the right time we will harvest a good crop if we don't give up, or quit" (Galatians 6:9, MSG). God is unyielding in God's love for us. Hebrews reminds us that God promised, "I will never leave you or forsake you" (13:5, NRSVUE). God's presence stubbornly remains with us when we get things right *and* when we mess things up. One of the many beautiful things

---

6. Richard Rohr, *The Universal Christ: How a Forgotten Reality Can Change Everything We See, Hope for, and Believe* (New York: Convergent, 2019), 15.

about God is that God never leaves us in our sin or mistakes but works through the Holy Spirit to redeem, and create new possibilities we could never imagine on our own.

Every Prayer and Tear Is Held in the Heart of God

Since we inhabit a world in which God is not only present to us but also constantly working in and through all creation, we can be confident that every prayer we speak, think, mutter, or groan contributes to God's restoration of all things in Christ. Our prayers do not need to be fully formed or elegantly articulated in order to count. We will "find ourselves," as N. T. Wright observes, "groaning in prayer, often without knowing exactly what we ought to be praying for, but then realizing—with Paul to remind us—that exactly there and then the Spirit is groaning within us, and the Father is listening, and that in the process we are being shaped according to the likeness of the beloved Son."[7]

No longing, desire, heartache, or tear is ever wasted in prayer. No prayers ever disappear. God hears and responds to every prayer, even when it seems there is no change in the person or circumstance for whom or which we pray. Every prayer we utter enters and is metabolized into the triune life of God. Let's unpack that.

God is always at work in the world. Even though it may seem as if our prayers float away on the wind and never find a home, a radical incarnational theology of prayer assures us that God hears, interprets, remembers, and responds to every sigh, longing, whimper, and sob ever uttered in the depths of our hearts. Because of the Spirit of God's radical presence and life within us, no prayer is ever lost. David offers a poignant image of this idea in Psalm 56, during a time when he has been seized by the Philistines. He fears for his life and prays to God, "You have kept count of my tossings; put my tears in your bottle. Are they not in

---

7. N. T. Wright, "Beginning to Think about the New Creation," N. T. Wright Online, https://www.ntwrightonline.org/beginning-to-think-about-the-new-creation.

your record?" (v. 8, NRSVUE). David is expressing the idea that God keeps track of our "every toss and turn through the sleepless nights" (v. 8, MSG). God never forgets our pain. Our prayers are never futile. They always remain present to the God who is always present to us and to the needs of all creation.

God places our tears in a bottle, and every heartache is entered into a ledger, where one day there will be a final accounting. God loves all of God's children. Our tears and pain touch the heart of God. Wherever there has been overwhelming pain, inexplicable evil, or injustice, we can rest assured that our experiences have also been experienced by God and have permanently entered the very life of the Trinity. In Revelation, we are promised that God will one day wipe these very tears from our eyes and that "'there will be no more death' or mourning or crying or pain, for the old order of things has passed away" (21:4).

Because the Spirit intercedes for us according to God's will (Romans 8:27), it is unlikely we will ever know the full ramifications of our prayers. "We never know when our prayers may help to lower all the thresholds of resistance in a complex social situation or when God may use our prayers to usher in some great divine purpose."[8] We keep praying in hope. We remain faithful, working and praying because the love of God sustains us. Hope leads us like the cloud that guided the Israelites by day and the pillar of fire by night.

What about Unanswered Prayer?

Like me, you may be wondering, *What about unanswered prayer?* Seeking to answer this question is personally painful because I've experienced many seemingly unanswered prayers over the years. I imagine you have as well. I will not offer formulas or sugarcoat this often avoided aspect of our life with God. It is unlikely we will

---

8. Jane E. Vennard and Stephen D. Bryant, *The Way of Prayer* (Nashville: Upper Room Books, 2007), 125.

ever fully understand why some prayers are miraculously answered while others meet with silence from God. For my own part, I admit that, even though some of my own heartfelt prayers have gone unanswered in the way I originally conceived them, God has often answered them in ways I never could have imagined (see Ephesians 3:20–21). Even in the midst of the deep and painful mystery of life, I keep trusting that God hears and responds to my prayers in ways that may remain largely unknowable in this present life.

There are many factors involved in the answering of prayer. Some of these are within our control, and others are not. Here are some of the things I keep in mind when I reflect on unanswered prayer or when I'm called to wait and persevere in prayer with no clear answer in sight. The following is not an exhaustive list, but it helps me keep things in theological perspective:

- God is working in every situation to the greatest extent possible for our well-being and the flourishing of all creation.
- While God's love is constant, unchanging, and faithful, it does not override human free will. People have free will and can thus respond to or reject God's gracious invitations.
- Human effort and hard work are needed for the answering of prayer. Prayer is not passive. Biblical prayer moves its feet. Authentic prayer engages in active service to others. We are often called to be the answer to our own prayers.
- Healthy relational skills are needed if relationships are to flourish. Prayer strengthens us and provides wisdom, but God also gives us important work that only we can do.
- Human limitation and trauma affect our capacity to respond to God's grace and to the love of others.
- The degree of health or severity of illness affect the efficacy of our prayers. For example, no one has ever regrown a leg lost in an accident. Many who have lost limbs, however, have gone on to live full lives.

- Genetic inheritance creates vulnerability to many physical and mental illnesses.
- Deeply embedded systemic issues affect our prayers, including cultural, social, historical, or political factors. These are what Paul referred to as the "principalities and powers" (Ephesians 6:12, KJV) of "this present darkness" (v. 12, NRSVUE).

All these factors help provide context for us to better understand what we're up against when our prayers are seemingly unanswered or the answers are delayed.

Incarnational Prayer Is Embodied in Justice

Because we cannot pray, love, or hope without bodies, our bodies are essential to fulfilling God's purposes in the world. Our prayers take on flesh as we work for justice. We pray when on our knees but also when we advocate for the vulnerable. Justice is what love looks like in action.[9] John Wesley put his prayers into action as he worked for prison reform, started orphanages and medical clinics, and visited the sick. Christ-centered prayer will lead us to "meet Jesus himself in the faces of the poor as in the parable of the sheep and the goats."[10] Teresa of Avila understood this truth centuries ago when she wrote: "Christ has no body now on earth but yours, no hands but yours, no feet but yours. Yours are the eyes through which Christ's compassion is to look out on the world. Yours are the feet with which Christ is to go about doing good. Yours are the hands with which Christ is to bless all people now."[11]

The closer we draw near to the heart of God in prayer, the more attuned to the injustices visited upon the marginalized we

---

9. I'm borrowing Cornel West's language here: "Justice is what love looks like in public." See https://traffickinginstitute.org/incontext-cornel-west/.

10. Wright, "Beginning to Think about the New Creation."

11. Cited in Vennard and Bryant, *The Way of Prayer*, 125–26.

will become. Brother Roger of Taizé expresses this concept well: "Prayer is a serene force at work within human beings, stirring them up, transforming them, never allowing them to close their eyes in the face of evil, of wars, of all that threatens the weak of this world."[12] We pray, but we also join hands with God to actively care for those in need. As my African friends remind me, "Prayer moves its feet." True prayer prods us to get up off our knees[13] and partner with God to become the answer to our own prayers. Saint Ignatius of Loyola is reported to have said, *Pray as if it all depends on God. Work as if it all depends on you.*

Putting Feet to Our Prayers

As a personal example of putting feet to my prayers, I have been praying for the healing of a compressed nerve in my back while I've been writing most of this book. The pain has often tested my resilience and distracted me from writing. I have talked to God about it, expressing my fears, frustrations, and anger about not being able to do everything I'm used to doing or staying on the writing schedule I set for myself. Along the way I have also sought a highly skilled, competent surgeon with a strong reputation. I understand that my part in seeking an answer to my prayer for healing involves doing what I can to maintain a healthier weight, exercise regularly, attend physical therapy, and do daily back-strengthening exercises. The practices of gratitude and hope certainly don't hurt either. A genuine answer to prayer involves all these things working together with the ever-present grace of God.

I eventually had back surgery—a laminectomy. I did well for the first ten days of recovery, but then I developed an infection at my surgical site, after which I underwent four weeks of antibiotics and was finally referred to a wound care clinic that performed two

---

12. Cited in Vennard and Bryant, *The Way of Prayer*, 50.
13. U2, "Please," *Pop* (Dublin, 1997).

debridements of my surgical site. The experience was incredibly painful and triggered traumatic memories from a bus accident I experienced in Ghana years ago while doing compassionate ministry work there. All of these factors made writing all but impossible for a couple of months. But life is like that sometimes, isn't it? None of us gets a free pass on trouble.

Perhaps another example will be helpful. If we are looking for healing in a relationship, we can rest assured that God will do what only God can do in strengthening our resolve, healing past hurts, and prompting hope for the future. But there is also a lot of work for us to do: growing in self-awareness, meeting with a counselor, confessing possible sins or hurts we have caused, learning new intimacy and relational skills, growing in listening skills and humility, and even restitution if we hurt someone deeply enough. God will help us with all these things, but it is a general biblical principle that we must respond after God calls. Remember, the Israelites had to put their feet in the waters of the Jordan River before the waters parted so they could pass over to the other side. And Peter was not able to walk on water until he got out of the boat.

If we expect God to heal us or answer the prayers of others without any effort on our part, then we're not really praying. We're invoking magic, not authentic prayer. Such false prayer is like rubbing a lamp and waiting for a genie to pop out and give us three wishes. When we pray like this, we make an idol out of the way we expect God to work in our lives. Wherever we see healing take place in the New Testament, God is always the healing agent yet always in response to trusting faith—even faith the size of a mustard seed.

Distorted Images of God

Distorted images of God can contribute to our growing weary in prayer. Perhaps such images come from our early experiences of learning about God. For example, there may be God the inner critic, who points out everything we do wrong. Or God the resident officer of the law, ready to charge and condemn us at every turn. Or maybe God the Santa Claus, ready to give us anything we desire. Or the God who rewards us when we do good and punishes us when we do bad—the subtext here being that God does not want to answer our prayers until we prove that we are worthy. If our prayers are not answered by this God, it's easy to blame ourselves.[14]

In any of these scenarios, we will find it difficult to pray with any degree of regularity. Intimacy with God will be difficult, indeed, when we are afraid to get too close to our distorted image of God because of the hurt it causes. It is no surprise that those who experience shame when they pray simply stop praying in meaningful ways. Then it becomes a negative feedback loop: the less we pray, the more shame we feel, and the more shame we feel, the less likely we are to draw near to God in prayer.

One of the biggest shifts in my own journey toward a more intimate relationship with God came out of the deep depression I talk about in a couple places in this book. Only as I experienced the overwhelming pain of depression was I able to let go of the distorted images of God I had constructed. In the midst of my deepest shame, I was finally able to embrace God's unconditional love of me—finally understanding that God loved me as much on my good days as on my bad days, that there was nothing I could do to make God love me more or less than God already loved me, that I did not have to achieve, accomplish, or be successful in order to earn God's love. The sheer fact that I *existed* was enough. *I* was enough. I was and am God's beloved, even when I didn't feel like it.

The Love of God Anchors Our Prayers

Our image of God determines whether we keep praying in difficult times or give up. Our image of God is thus the single

---

14. See J. B. Phillips's wonderful book *Your God Is Too Small* (New York: Touchstone, 2004) for examples of other distorted images of God.

most important factor when it comes to prayer. Roberta Bondi reminds us that "God's love is the starting point and ending point of prayer."[15] If we are to persevere in prayer and run our race well, the love of God must anchor us from start to finish. Bondi came to this same conclusion in her own prayer life:

> Before anything else, above all else, beyond everything else, God loves us. God loves us extravagantly, ridiculously, without limit or condition. God is in love with us. . . . God yearns for us. God does not love us 'in spite of who we are' or 'for whom God knows we can become.' . . . God loves us hopelessly as mothers love their babies. . . . God loves us, the very people we are; and not only that, but, even against what we ourselves sometimes find plausible, God likes us. . . . God loves me as God loves all people, without qualification. . . . What if, when God looks at God's children and what we do, God is struck first, not by all the awful things we [have done] but by God's love for us?[16]

This is exactly the kind of relationship for which God has created us in love. Who would not want to grow in a relationship with a God like this? Jane Vennard wisely points out, "This doesn't mean God likes everything we do or that God does not exercise judgment in love. It does mean that God desires above all else to be in a deep, abiding, growing relationship of love with us. Prayer is the expression of this relationship. We have been created for such communion."[17]

To fully embrace God's unconditional love from head to toe is the work of a lifetime. Regular prayer, meaningful worship, faithful friends, loving pastors, wise therapy, helpful books and podcasts, and spiritual directors can all be means of grace to promote healing of "the damaged image of God within us."[18] Roberta

---

15. Bondi, *In Ordinary Time: Healing the Wounds of Our Heart* (Nashville: Abingdon, 2001).

16. Bondi, *In Ordinary Time*, 22–23, 25, 32.

17. Vennard and Bryant, *The Way of Prayer*, 34.

18. Bondi, *In Ordinary Time*, 29.

Bondi's *In Ordinary Time* has been a means of grace in healing unloving images of God in my own life. I highly recommend it, especially if you find yourself in a similar place.

Pray without Ceasing

Since prayer is a personal relationship with God, then everything we do, say, or think has the potential to become prayer. As John Wesley put it, "All that a Christian does, even in eating and sleeping, is prayer when it is done in simplicity."[19] I love how he names two areas of life we might be least likely to connect to prayer: eating and sleeping. Even these, he says, are prayer. His point is that, whatever we do or say, we do it for the glory of God (see Colossians 3:17, 23). All of life has the potential to become worship and prayer. All of life can express and nurture a relationship with God. In my book *Healthy. Happy. Holy: 7 Practices toward a Holistic Life*, I discuss common elements of our lives that we do not often think of as counting when it comes to spiritual practices. These are such practices as attending to our own health, managing stress, engaging in play and hobbies, adequate sleep, regular exercise, and healthier eating. All of these are acts of worship, but they are also prayer in action.[20]

As I've grown in the practice and understanding of prayer, I've come to see that I pray in so many more ways than I used to give myself credit for. When I was a young Christian, I thought only structured times counted as authentic prayer. This mindset is similar to thinking that the only time we worship God is when we're at church. Worship at church is important, to be sure, but if the only time we worship God is at church, then our relationship

---

19. Wesley, *A Plain Account of Christian Perfection: Edited and Annotated by Randy L. Maddox and Paul W. Chilcote* (Kansas City, MO: Beacon Hill Press of Kansas City, 2015), 150.

20. See Joe Gorman, *Healthy. Happy. Holy: 7 Practices toward a Holistic Life* (Kansas City, MO: The Foundry Publishing, 2018).

with God is limited to a thin slice of life, indeed. We can be hard on ourselves when we think we don't pray enough, but most of us pray much more than we think we do. When we treat every aspect of our lives as worship, our whole lives can be prayer too.

When Paul told Thessalonians to "pray without ceasing" (1 Thessalonians 5:17), he wasn't laying an impossibly heavy burden on them. He was inviting them to recognize that everything they did had the potential to be prayer. Yes, prayer can be time specifically set aside for nurturing our relationship with God. But prayer can also be spontaneous: while sitting in a favorite chair or going for a walk, speaking words to God aloud or silently. More importantly, prayer is also our entire life lived faithfully before God, including our thoughts and our bodies.

Third-century theologian Origen helps us imagine a more holistic life of prayer: "Since the practice of virtue and the observance of the commandments form part of prayer, those who pray as well as work at the tasks they have to do, and combine their prayer with suitable activity, will be 'praying always.' This is the only way in which it is possible never to stop praying."[21] Origen is saying that prayer is embodied in our whole life: mind, heart, hands, feet. Everything we do, think, say, feel, experience, and enjoy can be a kind of prayer. In this understanding, prayer is not only centered in the mind, but it is also deeply embedded in our total selves, in every waking moment, and even when we are asleep.

Wendell Berry helps us embrace a more expansive understanding of prayer as well: "Sleep is the prayer the body prays."[22] What a gift to know that getting a good night's rest is an act of prayer! Prayer does not necessarily need to be words we consciously think or speak aloud. Prayer is something our bodies do as we move throughout our days.

---

21. Cited in Phyllis Tickle, *The Divine Hours: Prayers for Summertime* (New York: Doubleday, 2006), 18.

22. Berry, "Poem V, 1979," *A Timbered Choir: The Sabbath Poems 1979–1997* (Washington, DC: Counterpoint Press, 1998), 121.

Prayer is an expression of our entire life before God. If, at its heart, prayer is a personal relationship with God, then everything we do and say can be prayer. Jane Vennard and Stephen Bryant speak of whole-life prayer this way: "When we use our gifts and skills in the service of God with a lively sense of divine presence, we are praying. When we join God and others to create beauty, promote peace, or advocate for justice, we are praying."[23] As you develop a wider vision of prayer, you will see God at work in your life and in our world in ways perhaps you didn't before. You will find your internal reservoir filling up with joy, delight, and gratitude. You will develop a spring in your step and a twinkle in your eye. You will be more resilient and more flexible when the winds of adversity threaten to topple you.

Every time we respond to God's presence, we pray. This can be expressing gratitude for a beautiful sunset, the love we share with our family, the taste of a fresh strawberry. Prayer *is* words, but it is also so much more. When we come across a beautiful sight—a rose in bloom, fresh snow blanketing the ground, sparrows gleefully welcoming the day with loud songs of praise—and exclaim, "Wow, God! Thank you. Thank you. Thank you," in such moments when we feel a sense of the hush of standing on holy ground, *that* is prayer. Such gratitude goes down to the depths of our soul, welling up in a single syllable: *Wow!*

I love how Joyce Rupp describes these spontaneous moments of prayer:

> Praying does not always take place in a contained or predetermined place of reflection. We never know when there might be an interior turning toward the One who dwells with us and among us. Going for a walk or a run, stopping at night to bless sleeping children, driving past a homeless person, looking up to see a bright star in the heavens, receiving a note from a cherished friend, turning toward a spouse in pleasurable love, reading a

---

23. Vennard and Bryant, *The Way of Prayer*, 20.

story in the newspaper, hearing the pain in a colleague's anguish, waiting in a checkout line—at any time and any place we can be surprised and drawn into communion by the unanticipated sense of God's nearness.[24]

Praying Congregations and Resilience

One of the most important places we learn to pray is in church. A praying congregation boosts our resilience. As the body of Christ, we "mourn with those who mourn" and "rejoice with those who rejoice" (Romans 12:15). The solidarity we experience with one another, the sharing in each other's lives, is crucial to keeping our hope alive. I remember fondly the prayers of my church when I was a local pastor in Golden, Colorado. Their prayers sustained my family and me through some dark days as we journeyed with our daughter, Annie, in the early days of her chronic bone disease.[25]

On Wednesday nights, at what we called Kids' Club, we sang silly songs and serious songs. We shared Bible stories and did crafts with the kids. What surprised me was that the thing the kids most eagerly anticipated each week was sharing and then praying over our prayer requests. I've never seen anything like it, before or since. Their love for prayer as a group was totally unexpected. Many of them were not shy in praying in front of a group of up to twenty-five.

Many of the kids who attended Kids' Club did not attend church on Sunday mornings. As we slowly developed space for them in our Sunday morning service, what they most wanted to know was why we didn't share prayer requests on Sunday mornings like we did on Wednesday nights. Due to popular demand, I began opening up our Sunday morning congregational prayer time for spontaneous requests. At first, I was met with crickets.

24. Cited in Martin, *Learning to Pray*, 41.
25. I will tell more of Annie's story in a later chapter.

Many of the adults looked mortified that we'd do such a thing in the middle of a worship service. Then the kids jumped right in with their enthusiasm and transparency and, as a result, slowly led the adults to feel more comfortable sharing their own requests. As the lead pastor, these Wednesday and Sunday morning prayer times breathed life into me. These times became part of our church identity and influenced our entire congregation, building and shaping our individual and corporate resilience.

Another crucial place of prayer in that church was a "Companions in Christ" small group that met during the week.[26] Each week we took time to share prayer requests and pray for them as a group. Weekly, I wrote down the group's praises and requests on the inside flaps of the curriculum books we used. Throughout the writing of this chapter, I have looked back at many of those praises and requests in what has been a deeply moving experience. Some have died and are with God. The lives of many have turned out far more hopeful than we ever could have imagined at the time. As I read, I recognized clear answers to prayer that sometimes took several years to come about. As we shared requests and praises weekly, our vulnerability and intimacy with God and one another deepened. We felt safe to open up about our lives. We cried and celebrated together. The group still meets weekly, and has been doing so for more than twenty years now.

As I thumbed through the old books, I found the prayer request for Annie, then six, as she went through tests for muscular dystrophy. Those were some of the darkest days of my life, but I did not walk them alone. My Companions in Christ prayed, cried, and walked alongside us. Our lives became deeply entangled during our nearly twenty-one years with them. Even though I was the pastor, they also shepherded me. The authentic community I experienced in that group is a gift that continues to reverberate in my life. It's the reason I have dedicated this book to the faithful

---

26. *Companions in Christ* is a small group curriculum published by the Upper Room in Nashville.

folk at that church. Without their love, prayers, and faithfulness, it is unlikely I would be writing this book today.

FOR REFLECTION

- How would you finish these thoughts?
  - *I used to think of prayer primarily as . . .*
  - *But more and more I am coming to see it as . . .*
- What distorted ideas of God prevent you from praying fully and freely? What distorted images of God need to be healed in your life?
- What group experiences of prayer have been life-giving to you?
- How have you experienced praying without ceasing?
- Wendell Berry writes, "Sleep is the prayer the body prays." Sleep is not the only prayer the body prays. How would you fill in the blank?

_____ *is the prayer that the body prays.*

3

ANTS IN THE PANTS OF FAITH

In Praise of Doubt

RESILIENCE TIP

Resilient people learn to integrate faith and doubt in such a way that they are not seen as enemies but as companions who walk hand in hand on the journey of faith.

Be merciful to those who doubt.

—Jude 1:22

If God's reality could be proved to anyone beyond a doubt, like the indisputable evidence in a laboratory experiment, there would be no room for doubt, and thus no room for faith.

—Michael Lodahl, The Story of God

Doubts are the ants in the pants of faith. They keep it awake and moving.

—Frederick Buechner, Wishful Thinking

It may be that when we no longer know what to do we have come to our real work, and that when we no longer know which way to go we have come to our real journey. The mind that is not baffled is not employed. The impeded stream is the one that sings.

—Wendell Berry, "The Real Work"

The experience of doubt is essential to living a fully alive Christian life. At the same time, doubt is an issue many of us don't want to talk about, let alone admit we experience it. Doubt is painful. We deny it and try to shove it into the back of our mind, thinking it might disappear if we don't acknowledge its presence. But genuine doubt is the elephant in the room for many in the church. It lurks in the shadows during the day and haunts us at night. We feel ashamed of experiencing doubt. "Good Christians shouldn't doubt," we scold ourselves. Sharing our doubt with others can feel like confessing an unforgivable sin.

We may find ourselves in the clutches of doubt for many reasons. It can be due to unanswered prayer, unremitting health issues, relational difficulties, divorce, death of a loved one, or even deep disappointment in the gulf between what Christ's church says it believes and how it actually follows Christ in the world. As a pastor and college professor, I have talked with many sincere Christ followers who have experienced unrelenting doubt. Many feel deep shame about what they perceive as their inability to trust fully in God. Others have been taught that doubt is destructive to faith and even a sin. The purpose of this chapter is to show that doubt can be an impetus to deeper faith and confidence in Christ. How we view and respond to doubt makes all the difference in how we run our God-given race.

College Students and Doubt

Many of the college students I teach experience severe doubt. Most often, they bring their doubts with them to college. Sometimes professors are accused of "deconstructing" the faith of college students. Nothing could be further from the truth. A lot of religion professors at Christian universities are ordained clergy. Our calling and passion is to see our students grow into the full stature of Christ. God has called us to build up students in their faith, not tear it apart. We want them to be resilient, faithful, creative, and redemptive ambassadors for Christ in the world.

Because many of the students in the Introduction to Theology class I teach every year have shared their doubts with me, I now include a brief lecture early in the semester on the role of doubt in the life of sincere Christ followers. In response to this lecture, many students have told me that they have previously had no safe place to express their doubts or ask questions. Some have even been told by those in their home churches to quit asking so many questions. It breaks my heart every time I hear such revelations from a student.

Many young people have been raised with the idea that it's bad to doubt. They have been told that faith and doubt oppose each other. As a result, many feel shame about their doubts. Getting their theology straight about the role of doubt in developing an authentic faith is a big relief to them. At the end of each semester, I ask my Intro to Theology students to share three main takeaways from the course. Of the many topics we explore throughout the semester, the one that appears most often in course evaluations is how students have grown in their understanding of the relationship between faith and doubt. Here are a couple examples of what students have written:

This course has reaffirmed to me that God is love and we do not need to have all the answers. One of the concepts covered in class that has stuck with me the most is where doubt fits in with faith. Previously, I was told and felt as though doubt had no place in my faith. I did not feel comfortable telling God about the places I couldn't understand. However, in our class discussions, it was said that doubt can make us stronger because it means we are actually seeking God and his truth instead of taking what others say as true without question. As a result of this course, I have found myself being more open with God and not feeling shame about my questions, doubts, and fears. God is good, God is love, and God can handle my questions.

Another student wrote, "When I had a lot of doubts about God while growing up, I felt guilty because I thought we weren't allowed to ask questions or have doubts. This class has helped me to realize that questions and even doubt are good and can help me grow deeper in my faith and relationship with God."

My Doubt as a College Freshman

I experienced a full-blown case of doubt as a college freshman several months after I became a Christian. Wanting to learn more about my faith and that of others, I took a World Religions class at the local community college. Unfortunately, the course was taught by an embittered professor who ridiculed all faiths, especially any faith we brought with us into the class.[1] As the semester progressed, I descended into a deep pit of doubt. It was a devastating season of life for my newborn faith. I wondered if I might be like the seed that fell on rocky ground in Jesus's parable of the sower: "Others, like seed sown on rocky places, hear the word and at once receive it with joy. But since they have no root, they last only a short time. When trouble or persecution comes because of the word, they quickly fall away" (Mark 4:16–17). I have since learned that rootedness and resilience are intimately related. The doubt I experienced from this class was not the fault of the subject matter. I was particularly vulnerable as a young Christian, and the professor for the course obviously enjoyed being a provocateur. I later took additional world religions courses at other schools and found my faith affirmed, as well as encouragement to develop a more generous spirit toward other faiths.

---

1. Those within the Wesleyan theological tradition acknowledge that God's prevenient grace is active in all religions. This does not mean one religion is as good as any other but that whenever we find faith, hope, and love, we can rest assured it comes from the presence of the Trinity. Jesus will always be "the way, the truth, and the life" (see John 14:6) for Christians. Wesleyans sometimes refer to this view as "a wider hope." See Charles R. Gailey and Howard Culbertson, *Discovering Missions* (Kansas City, MO: Beacon Hill Press of Kansas City, 2007).

Just as the depth of our roots can determine the strength of our resilience, so also the depth of our doubt can determine the strength of our faith. Mark Buchanan says so well, "Perhaps this is a general principle: the depth of our doubt is roughly proportionate to the depth of our faith. Those with strong faith have equally strong doubts. That principle bears out in the other direction as well: people with a trivial and shallow faith usually have trivial and shallow doubts."[2] These words have resonated with me for many years. Rather than our doubts revealing our lack of faith, they can contribute to the depth of our faith.

Several months after that first world religions class was over, when my faith was at a low ebb, my pastor opened the altar for prayer after a sermon. It was as if two hands lifted me out of my seat and led me to the altar, where several friends surrounded me in prayer. My doubts didn't instantly disappear, but this time of prayer in the company of other Christians was a defining moment for me. I began to ask myself, *Am I going to cave into my doubts or rise up courageously, trusting that God really is with me, whether I sense God or not?* It was a tough lesson to learn as a young Christian.

The pain of those doubts as an eighteen-year-old provoked me to dig deeper into my faith. I was not raised in the church, so I knew almost nothing about Jesus when I first stepped foot inside a church. I did not know Genesis from Revelation. I knew Jesus had died on a cross because my grandparents had a crucifixion painting hanging above their television, but I knew nothing about the resurrection. Easter was about bunnies, chocolate, and family picnics. I had a lot of catching up to do. My insatiable desire to learn more about my faith led me to read through the entire Bible in less than a year. I visited my local Christian bookstore and began to devour books that helped me grow in confidence about the reliability of the Bible and the historical trustworthiness

---

2. Mark Buchanan, "The Benefit of the Doubt," *Christianity Today*, April 2000, 64.

of Jesus's death and resurrection. By God's grace, I slowly learned to manage my doubts and grow deeper spiritual roots.

After receiving a call into ministry, I enrolled in a Christian college as a sophomore and declared a ministry major. During those years, I began to discover the huge difference between doubting God and doubting *my understanding* of God. There were many times when I felt like I was losing my faith. In reality, I was finding my former understandings of God to be inadequate. The trouble was that my God was too small.[3] I clung to my previous understandings of God with white knuckles. Only with great pain was I able to let go of those old, inadequate, misleading, toxic ideas of God to embrace a more Christlike God. Christian Wiman speaks of the difficulty of letting toxic beliefs go: "How astonishing it is, the fierceness with which we cling to beliefs that have made us miserable, or beliefs that prove to be so obviously inadequate when extreme suffering—or great joy—come. . . . The greatest tragedy of human existence is not to live in time, in both senses of that phrase."[4]

One of my favorite biblical stories about putting God in a box comes from Jonah. At the beginning of the book, the love of Jonah's God only extends to those who are like him. As Jonah flees from God on a ship, a great storm arises. The sailors blame Jonah for it, and he is thrown overboard to drown. God sends a whale to "rescue" Jonah. He spends three days in its belly, after which even the whale has had enough of him and spits Jonah up onto the shore. I always want to ask Jonah at this point, "Do you hurt enough, or do you need to hurt a little more to understand the expansive love of God?" It begins to dawn on Jonah that his God is indeed too small, too narrow, too tribal. Slowly and painfully he considers that he might have created God in his own image. Eventually he confesses that he has shrunk God down to

---

3. J. B. Phillips's *Your God Is Too Small* (1952) was helpful to me during this time.

4. Christian Wiman, *My Bright Abyss: Meditation of a Modern Believer* (New York: Farrar, Straus and Giroux, 2013), 8.

his size and repents—but with a poor attitude. Anne Lamott's observation applies well to Jonah, and to all of us whose gods may be far too small and unChristlike: "You can safely assume you've created God in your own image when it turns out that God hates all the same people you do."[5]

Doubt Is a Normal Part of a Vibrant Faith

A crucial part of growing beyond nagging doubt is to acknowledge it as a normal part of faith development.[6] When we catastrophize doubt, its hold on us grows in intensity. When we normalize doubt and uncertainty on the journey of faith, they lose a great deal of power. Psychologist Susan David's research shows that denying difficult emotions can actually make them stronger in a phenomenon known as "the amplification effect."[7] When we acknowledge and normalize experiences like doubt, we lessen their grip on us. Stuart Henderson's poem "I Believe" helps us normalize the role of doubt in a growing faith:

I believe in doubt
I believe doubt is a process of saying
"Excuse me, I have a question."[8]

The experience of doubt asks us to pay attention to it. For example, I might have a conversation like the following with myself: *I notice I'm experiencing doubt. Where is it coming from? What's going on in my life that may be contributing to my feelings of doubt? God, what can I learn from this season of doubt?* The

---

5. Lamott, *Bird by Bird*, 22.

6. See Janet O. Hagberg and Robert A. Guelich, *The Critical Journey: Stages in the Life of Faith* (Salem, WI: Sheffield Publishing Company, 2005).

7. Susan David, "The Tyranny of Positivity," Emotional Agility Newsletter, July 2021, https://www.susandavid.com/newsletter/.

8. Stuart Henderson, "I Believe," in Pádraig Ó Tuama, *Daily Prayer with the Corrymeela Community* (London: Canterbury Press, 2017).

experience of doubt is like a smoke detector. Rather than signaling the end of our faith, it signals that something is going on that we need to pay attention to. We can attend to it by taking it to God in prayer or by talking it over with a trusted friend or mentor.

Perhaps surprisingly, doubt can be a form of prayer. Just as psalms of lament are an integral part of a vibrant prayer life, so is doubt an essential part of an honest, vulnerable, thriving relationship with God. If doubt is a form of lament offered to God in honest prayer, then it is a sign of the *presence* rather than the *absence* of faith. Doubt does not need to be an obstacle to resilience. It can actually be a doorway to a deeper, more vibrant faith as it spurs us to grow in our relationship with God and others.

Doubt Is Holistic

Doubt is a complex phenomenon with strands of faith, theology, emotion, and character woven together. As an emotion, it is simply data—information about how we are feeling in a given moment. In this sense, it is neither good nor bad. Doubt as an emotion tells us how we are navigating life. When we sense ourselves entering a period of doubt, rather than chastising ourselves for our perceived lack of faith, why not simply say, "I notice I'm experiencing doubt." Spoken this way, we can calmly acknowledge that yes, we are experiencing doubt. In this way we're less likely to catastrophize our doubts and will instead be able to lean into them and figure out what they may be able to teach us. I've found that questions like these help me during times of doubt:

- What can I learn from this season of doubt?
  - *God, help me view this doubt as a gracious invitation from you to press on in my relationship with you rather than to see it as a sign of my falling away from you.*
- Are there particular reasons I'm feeling doubtful?

— *Perhaps someone criticized me, a prayer has gone unanswered, someone I love died too young, I lost a job, or I was passed over at work.*

- How can this period of doubt lead me to growth in prayer and intimacy with God?
   — *Perhaps I need to explore new forms of prayer, listen to sermons and podcasts, or read books that talk about intimacy with God in the midst of doubt.*[9]

Christian faith is not a once-and-done journey. As we grow in any significant relationship or area of life, there will be growing pains. As Christ followers, we're always on the way, forever in process, continually growing, even though at times we may feel stuck. For those who locate themselves in the Wesleyan-Holiness tradition, there is an important message here for living a life of Christlikeness: Christlike holiness is not a static, finished experience. It is a dynamic, lifetime journey of new surrenders, fresh challenges, unanticipated growth, and also one with setbacks, failures, and doubts along the way.

A Thriving Faith Needs Doubt

It has taken a long time, but I have eventually come to a place of relative peace with doubt. I no longer view doubt as an enemy but as a companion on the journey of faith. On my best days I do not resist or fight feelings of doubt, which has relieved doubt of much of its power in my life. When I no longer view doubt as an enemy, I am able to see it as one of God's angelic messengers leading me to a deeper and more vibrant life of faith

---

9. The experience of doubt can be a season of life that is sometimes referred to among those who study Christian spiritual formation as a "dark night of the soul." Saint John of the Cross, a sixteenth-century Spanish priest and mystic, wrote the classic book on the experience of the dark night of the soul. See *Dark Night of the Soul*, trans. Mirabai Starr (New York: Riverhead Books, 2003).

and prayer. It makes all the difference how we view doubt: is it an enemy to fight and overcome at all costs? Or is it a tough, difficult teacher, even a friend? The language we use about doubt reveals our core beliefs about it. We often use words like "falling," "slipping," "backsliding," or "losing faith." The redemptive role of doubt is difficult to see in such language. What about using words like "friend," "companion," "growth," "opportunity," or "deeper faith" instead?

Doubt is an honest response to the pain and bewilderment of life. It is not the opposite of faith. Anne Lamott offers a key corrective to our conventional wisdom regarding the relationship between faith and doubt: "The opposite of faith is not doubt, but certainty. Certainty is missing the point entirely. Faith includes noticing the mess, the emptiness and discomfort, and letting it be there until some light returns. Faith also means reaching deeply within, for the sense one was born with, the sense, for example, to go for a walk."[10] God enables us to hold faith and doubt together, simultaneously. They are two sides of the same coin. Rather than being in opposition to each other, they complement each other. Instead of speaking of doubt as the opposite of faith, why don't we speak of it as the other side of faith? Our aim as Christians is for a faith that trusts. We keep walking in trust even if we don't see the way ahead or when the road before us is littered with pot-holes. The word "certainty" pertains to mathematical theorems, not personal relationships. It is a category mistake to speak of certainty in any relationship. I speak of the loving relationship I have with my wife, not of my absolute certainty in the truth of our marriage.

As the apostle Paul reminds us, "For we live by faith, not by sight" (2 Corinthians 5:7). Faith has to do with a trusting relationship, whereas sight has to do with certainty. The search for certainty will lead us astray, resulting in arrogance and division,

---

10. Lamott, *Plan B: Further Thoughts on Faith* (New York: Riverhead Books, 2006), 257.

possibly even violence. A faith that has some doubt sprinkled in is a humble faith, acknowledging that it is limited, perspectival, and shaped by its cultural and social location. I fear for those who believe in Christ without any doubts. With no doubt, there's no room for humility. There's no space to be wrong. It's too easy to be coercive and even violent in our certainty. We can be so absolutely convinced of our ideas that we do not know how to take no for an answer. Far too often we see the destruction absolute certainty wreaks in our world.

John Wesley understood firsthand the damage lack of humility can cause among Christians. In his context in eighteenth-century England, there were battles over the right kind of worship. His sermon "Catholic Spirit" was a response to the divisiveness he saw among Christians. The word "Catholic" does not refer to the Roman Catholic Church but to the church universal, Christ's church throughout the world. One of the key phrases in this sermon, whose message is much needed in our day is, "Though we cannot think alike, may we not love alike?"[11] Humble faith is loving and hospitable toward other opinions. Generosity of spirt heals. Certainty wounds. Absolute certainty kills. Next time you are tempted to get mad at someone you love even though you disagree with them over faith or politics, I encourage you to repeat Wesley's words to yourself: *Though we cannot think alike, may we not love alike?*

Faith and doubt go together like faith and works. It's not faith *or* works but a faith *that* works. Similarly, it's not that we *either* have faith *or* we doubt but that we have a faith that both trusts *and* doubts. Both trust and doubt are essential to a thriving Christian life. Addressing the presence of doubt in our lives is a crucial practice for those who seek to strengthen the grip of resilience on their lives.

---

11. John Wesley, "Sermon 39: Catholic Spirit," http://wesley.nnu.edu/john-wesley/the-sermons-of-john-wesley-1872-edition/sermon-39-catholic-spirit/. See also Dan Boone's excellent books on the topic of loving while disagreeing, *A Charitable Discourse: Talking about the Things That Divide Us* (2011) and *A Charitable Discourse, Volume 2: Uncomfortable Conversations* (2016), both available from The Foundry Publishing.

Doubt, like pain, can be an agent of change. We change not so much when we see the light but when we feel the heat. Like most avenues to growth, it may be painful but is well worth it in the end. Without the experience of doubt to prod us, how likely are we to press on and learn about new subjects or read authors who may stretch us and offer a new understanding of Scripture and Christian faith? Left to our own devices, we will remain with the comfortable and predictable. The human default setting is homeostasis.

Doubt is unsettling. It forces us to reconsider our usual ways of thinking about and relating to God. The more persistent and painful our doubt, the more likely we are to begin to explore new paths on the road of faith. I love Frederick Buechner's humorous insight on this subject that gave us the title for this chapter: "Whether your faith is that there is a God or that there is not a God, if you don't have any doubts, you are either kidding yourself or asleep. Doubts are the ants in the pants of faith. They keep it awake and moving."[12] Doubts keep us reaching, learning, discovering, moving, dancing, and growing.

What Does the Bible Say about Doubt?

As I mentioned in the introduction to this book, the history of Israel and of the early church is largely one of steadfast resilience in the face of overwhelming obstacles and setbacks. Similarly, we see doubt lived out in the lives of many of our most beloved characters in Scripture. Doubt has been among us for as long as human beings have been following God. We are finite and limited. We will never be able to wrap our minds fully around the holy mystery of God. It's like trying to pour all the world's oceans into a thimble. It simply cannot be done. Here are some examples of scriptural doubt:

---

12. Buechner, *Wishful Thinking*, 20.

- Israel was unable to sense God's presence because of their despair and cruel bondage (Exodus 6:9).
- To the consternation of his friends, Job refused to keep his questions and doubts to himself (see Job 3–26).
- Israel doubted God's love (Malachi 1:2).
- It may sound heretical, but even Jesus doubted. Frederick Buechner says, "When he cried out, 'My God, my God, why hast thou forsaken me!' I don't think he was raising a theological issue any more than he was quoting Psalm 22. I think he had looked into the abyss itself and found there a darkness that spiritually, viscerally, totally engulfed him."[13] If even Jesus doubted, then perhaps we can be easier on ourselves when we doubt.
- The two despair-filled disciples on the road to Emmaus expressed their doubt to the unrecognized, resurrected Christ: "But we had hoped that he [Jesus] was the one who was going to redeem Israel" (Luke 24:21).
- The disciples did not immediately recognize the resurrected Jesus: "When they saw him, they worshiped him; but some doubted" (Matthew 28:17). Matthew doesn't act as if they sinned by doubting. He includes the words "some doubted" as if doubt in this situation were the most natural thing in the world.
- "Be merciful to those who doubt" (Jude 1:22). Jude drops this gem of inspired wisdom at the end of his short letter. The book of Jude was written to encourage co-laborers in Christ to persevere, to keep them from stumbling (v. 24). The letter speaks of "building yourselves up in your most holy faith and praying in the Holy Spirit" (v. 20). It tells them to "keep yourselves in God's love" (21) as a means of forming resilience in the face of the obstacles to faith that

---

13. Buechner, *Wishful Thinking*, 20.

community was facing. Like Jude, may we be gentle toward those who doubt, including ourselves.

Christlike disciples are not people who never doubt. They are those who doubt and worship, doubt and pray, doubt and serve, doubt and love. They have learned to embrace the experience of doubt and help others with their doubts. To be a community where everybody can be vulnerable about their faith *and* their doubts is who we, as the body of Christ, are called to be.

Doubting Thomas

The patron saint of doubt is, of course, the disciple Thomas. We show our bias against doubt by giving him the pejorative nickname "Doubting Thomas." But why do we pick on Thomas and not other characters in the New Testament, like "Needy Nicodemus or Codependent Martha"?[14] And Thomas clearly isn't the only disciple of Jesus ever to have doubted (see Matthew 28:17; Mark 16:14; Luke 24:11, 25, 37–38, 41, among other examples).

After the disciples report Jesus's resurrection to Thomas, he is resistant (John 20:25). He's heard Peter spout outlandish things before. This isn't his first rodeo with the rest of the disciples either. It is reasonable that he wants to see and touch the evidence for himself. Another thing I admire about Thomas is that he has the courage to say what others are probably thinking but too afraid to admit.

The truth is, we've been too quick to judge Thomas. The episode we encounter in John 20 is one short glimpse of Thomas. It's one moment in time, a "single story,"[15] a snapshot of grief-induced

---

14. Nadia Bolz-Weber, "Doubt," *The Corners* (April 11, 2021), https://thecorners. substack.com/p/doubt.

15. If you have not seen the brilliant TED Talk "The Danger of a Single Story," by Chimamanda Ngozi Adichie, you owe it to yourself to watch it: https://www.ted.com/ talks/chimamanda_ngozi_adichie_the_danger_of_a_single_story. Here is the description

doubt in a complex life of faithfulness. We can easily get tripped up when we reduce anyone's character or relationship with God to a single event or season of life. Our lives are never that simple. Each of us is so much more than our worst moments. Thomas's doubt is ours. Like Thomas, our doubts are not the only thing to know about us.

I love that Jesus doesn't judge or label Thomas. Jesus does not cast him away because of his doubts but invites him to see the wounds and touch his flesh. We don't know if Thomas ever actually did touch Jesus's wounds. We only know Jesus did not shame, ridicule, or mock Thomas. Jesus received all of the disciples in the midst of their unspoken doubts, fears, and shame—and he continues to do the same with us.

John Wesley and Doubt

Even John Wesley, the founder of what we call the Methodist movement, had times of serious doubt. When I was working on my doctoral dissertation about pastors, burnout, and depression, I came across several places in Wesley's diaries where he spoke of his doubts and even depression.[16] In a journal entry that was occasioned by Wesley's receipt of a letter from Oxford regarding the relationship between faith and doubt, he wrote that he was thrown "into much perplexity." The message of the letter was that doubt of any kind was incompatible with true faith. The implication was that, as Wesley says, "whoever at any time felt any doubt or fear was not *weak in faith*, but had *no faith* at all." After begging God to direct his mind to Scripture for an answer

of her talk from the TED website: "Our lives, our cultures, are composed of many overlapping stories. Novelist Chimamanda Adichie tells the story of how she found her authentic cultural voice—and warns that if we hear only a single story about another person or country, we risk a critical misunderstanding." I would add that we also risk judging rather than loving others.

16. In the course of my research I also learned of the depression of Martin Luther, Charles Spurgeon, J. B. Phillips, Henri Nouwen, and more.

to his dilemma, he came upon some verses that reassured him that even biblical heroes had doubts but still possessed faith. He concludes his journal entry with these words: "After some hours spent in the Scripture and prayer I was much comforted. Yet I felt a kind of soreness in my heart, so that I found my wound was not fully healed. O God, save thou me, and all that are 'weak in the faith,' from 'doubtful disputations.'"[17]

Even the mature Wesley continued to experience doubt from time to time. The following was written to his brother Charles during a tumultuous time in his ministry:

> [I do not love God. I never did]. Therefore [I never] believed in the Christian sense of the word. Therefore [I am only an] honest heathen, a proselyte of the Temple, one of the [God-fearers]. And yet to be so employed of God! and so hedged in that I can neither get forward nor backward! Surely there never was such an instance before, from the beginning of the world! If I [had ever had] *that faith*, it would not be so strange. But [I never had any] other [evidence] of the eternal or invisible world than [I have] now; and that is [none at all], unless such as faintly shines from reason's glimmering ray. [I have no] direct witness, I do not say that [I am a child of God], but of anything invisible or eternal.[18]

These writings help us see that, although John Wesley is a model for many of us in our journeys with God, his faith was not simplistic, serene, or trouble-free. Wesley was a gifted person,

---

17. Wesley, June 6, 1738, *Bicentennial Edition of the Works of John Wesley*, 18:254.
18. Wesley, Letter to Charles Wesley, June 27, 1766, cited in Richard P. Heitzenrater, *The Elusive Mr. Wesley: John Wesley His Own Biographer*, Vol. 1 (Nashville: Abingdon, 1984), 198–99. During this season of Wesley's life, as Heitzenrater notes, "the Methodist movement was experiencing a great deal of upheaval and tension." The editors of Wesley's letters make this comment about the brackets found in the letters of Wesley: "We keep editorial additions to the text of letters at a minimum, and clearly identify them with [square brackets]. A few of the manuscript sources have been damaged or have obscured text. In these cases we have reconstructed the missing text as much as possible, placing the reconstructed text within ‹angled brackets›." See https://wesley-works.org/editorial-guidelines.

yet he was as human as you and I. Far from his life being one unbroken chain of successes and spiritual victories, he failed, he hurt, he questioned, and he doubted. But he continued to look to God in prayer, Scripture, the sacraments, and other people. This picture of Wesley is within our reach. We can relate to it, and it can help us normalize our own seasons of doubt.

Approaching the Bible for Its Questions Rather than Its Answers

Doubt has taught me to embrace the questions that come my way. Rainer Maria Rilke's words help me be gentle with myself when I'm impatient for answers:

> I would like to beg of you, dear friend, as well as I can, to have patience with everything that remains unsolved in your heart. Try to love the *questions themselves*, like locked rooms and like books written in a foreign language. Do not now look for answers. They cannot now be given to you because you could not live them. It is a question of experiencing everything. At present you need to *live* the questions. Perhaps you will gradually, without even noticing it, find yourself experiencing the answer, some distant day.[19]

Rilke is not saying we should never seek adequate responses to our questions but that there are seasons of life when we need to sit with the questions, listen to them, embrace them, wrestle with them, and lament when there are no answers for loss or pain.

So often we "kick against the goads" (Acts 26:14) when experiencing doubt. A goad is a long, sharp stick that was used in ancient times to guide livestock. The contemporary English paraphrase might be, "So often we kick and scream when we don't get our way or things don't turn out the way we planned."

---

19. Rainer Maria Rilke, *Letters to a Young Poet*, trans. Joan M. Burnham (Novato, CA: New World Library, 1992), 35.

Counterintuitively, in times like these, we need to "live the questions," embrace our pain, accept our situation, or befriend our thorn in the flesh (see 2 Corinthians 12:7).

Walking with Doubt

I share the following about my own journey with doubt in the hopes that it can normalize the doubt you may experience, as well as give you hope that a better day will come.

Our daughter, Annie, has a chronic bone disease called pseudo-rheumatoid condra-dysplasia. The disease mimics rheumatoid arthritis in some ways but biologically is very different. Its constant and unrelenting pain can only be lessened through high-powered painkillers and surgery. Shelly and I first noticed that something was going on with Annie's joints when she was two years old and her feet started to turn severely inward. She had her first major surgery at the age of five, a bilateral, de-rotational osteotomy to turn her feet outward, giving her the best chance possible of walking. She started kindergarten in a wheelchair with purple, candy-cane-striped casts that went from her toes to her hips.

When Annie was seven, one of her doctors thought she might have muscular dystrophy and ordered a biopsy of a muscle in her thigh. The five days Shelly and I waited for the test results from that biopsy were the longest we have ever endured. Waves of fear swept over us as we contemplated what might come to be. During these days, Shelly and I couldn't help but mourn Annie's early death. Many children with muscular dystrophy do not live past their early twenties. I walked around with what felt like a hundred-pound weight on my chest. Though I'm not normally a crying person, I cried every time I thought of Annie—which was most of the time.

The biopsy was on a Thursday. I was a local church pastor in Colorado at the time. My thoughts were so consumed with dark doubts about Annie's future that I was afraid I would be unable to come up with a sermon for Sunday. I somehow managed to come up with a short sermon on Jesus's proclamation from the cross, "I thirst." What I really felt like preaching on were Jesus's final words from the cross, "My God, my God, why have you forsaken me?" but thought better of it. I felt like I was hanging on my own cross with no hope of resurrection. God seemed a million miles away. I somehow led the service that Sunday without breaking down. When it came time for the sermon, I stumbled for words but somehow managed to share with the church about Annie's possible diagnosis. After that I didn't know what else to do, so I went to the altar and fell on my knees while the church surrounded Shelly and me with their love and prayers. I have never felt more utterly weak and hopeless.

On the following Tuesday we found out that Annie did not have muscular dystrophy. We felt as if our daughter, just like Jairus's daughter, had been raised from the dead (see Mark 5:21–24, 35–43). It was a day of celebration even though many other painful days followed in its wake. Even so, our celebration was muted because we knew that far too many families receive the worst of the worst news in situations like these. Journeying with Annie's bone disease has taught us to celebrate whatever small victories occur because we never know when the next tsunami may hit.

As I write this, I ask myself, *How can I as a father possibly talk about my daughter's pain?* Annie's bone disease is not mine. I don't feel daily, excruciating, mind-numbing pain in my hips, knees, back, shoulders, or neck. Yet I do feel her pain. Shelly and I have deeply felt Annie's pain as we have walked alongside her through more than thirteen major surgeries, countless doctor's appointments, and hundreds of hours of physical therapy.

"Vicarious trauma" is the term psychology has coined for secondhand pain. Vicarious trauma is like inhaling secondhand smoke. We aren't the one smoking, yet we may become ill as a result of our close proximity to those who are. Shelly and I have felt Annie's pain in our bodies. We have been physically exhausted and emotionally spent after her many surgeries. When she has a bad day, we feel it in our bones. We have been traumatized by Annie's bone disease right alongside her. It's not Annie's fault. It's just the way we humans are when we love. A child's pain is not something parents can cordon off from the rest of our lives. We can't fence it off in the back of our minds and go about our days as if nothing is wrong. Our children's pain affects our ability to see hope, experience delight, or do ministry.

One of my most enduring memories of Annie's journey with chronic pain comes from when she was eleven years old in the fifth grade. I was waiting for her in the disabled parking spot at her elementary school. She had called and asked through tears if I could pick her up early because she was hurting so badly. The doors of the school opened. Annie, on crutches, began painstakingly shuffling down the sidewalk to where I was waiting. As she got closer, I could see the excruciating pain written on her face, tears streaming down her cheeks. Her body was wracked with pain at every step she took. I knew she did not want me to help her, lest one of the other kids might see. Like so many other times, I was powerless to take my daughter's pain away.

Shortly after this, Annie gave up walking as too painful, a devastating development for all of us. It was the death of yet another hope we'd had for Annie. Every parent eagerly awaits the day when their child will take their first step—and then assumes their child will continue to walk through their entire lives. During this season of life, any hope we had of Annie ever walking again died. Annie's bone disease had progressed to the point that chunks of cartilage were breaking off and getting stuck in her hip and knee joints, causing excruciating pain, so we purchased a mobility scooter for her.

Before Annie transitioned to a mobility scooter, I had been traveling to teach at Africa Nazarene University for a month every summer. Once Annie could no longer walk, I put a pause on my trips. Shelly worked a demanding full-time job at a local hospital, and our son was not old enough to drive Annie to her various appointments. I was what we liked to call back then the "PoD"—parent on duty.

The vicarious trauma Shelly and I experienced caring for Annie and just getting her through the day was overwhelming at times. As any parent of a child with a disability knows, there are no days off. Shelly and I were not exempt from the dark and sometimes hopeless road we had been given to walk. And sometimes we didn't walk. We limped and crawled through some days as best we could. And, since Annie's physical challenges continue to this day, there are times when we still do. Shelly and I were often full of doubts regarding God's presence during those early years. Anyone who has watched their child suffer deeply and persistently cannot help but doubt God's presence. Why had God allowed this disease to take over Annie's life? Did God hear our prayers to at least lessen her pain? Why was God allowing her to experience so much suffering? Seeing Annie sobbing, her body wracked with pain, hour after hour with no end in sight, was physically and spiritually traumatizing. Stanley Hauerwas summarizes my thoughts well: "It is speculatively interesting to ask how the existence of a good and all-powerful God can be reconciled with the existence of evil in the world. . . . But when I confront the actual suffering and threatened death of my child—such speculative considerations grounding belief or unbelief seem hollow."[20]

Annie was thirteen when she had double hip-and-knee-replacement surgery. Two surgeries, three months apart, and then the long, painful journey of recovery and physical therapy were upon us. Shelly and I did not believe Annie would ever walk again after these surgeries. Our humble hope was that the surgeries would lessen her pain. Several years had gone by since Annie had last walked more than a few steps at a time. It

---

20. Stanley Hauerwas, *Naming the Silences: God, Medicine, and the Problem of Suffering* (Grand Rapids: Eerdmans, 1990), 1.

seemed like far too much of a reach to believe she would ever walk again. I can't help but think of the Emmaus Road disciples who poured out their grief to the unrecognized, resurrected Christ: "We had hoped" (Luke 24:21). Like the Israelites suffering under Egyptian slavery, it was difficult to hear God's voice or sense God's presence "because of [our] broken spirit" (Exodus 6:9, NRSVUE).

In the midst of our doubt and brokenness, out of nowhere, our dear friend Caritas from Gisenyi, Rwanda, emailed us to let us know she had organized an event called Annie Walking Day at their church in Rwanda. I had met Caritas and her husband, Simon Pierre, through one of the students I taught at Africa Nazarene University. Over the years I stayed with Simon Pierre, Caritas, and their children many times in between teaching classes in Kenya and doing compassionate ministry work in Rwanda and the Democratic Republic of Congo. My church had also partnered with them on several compassionate ministry projects. Simon Pierre stayed in our home in Colorado several times while traveling in the U.S., which is how he met and got to know Annie; he later told Caritas about her bone disease.

Caritas proudly told me their entire church had paraded throughout the Gisenyi community, praying that Annie would walk again. I was deeply grateful for Caritas's prayers and her efforts in gathering the church to pray. I remember thinking, *It certainly couldn't hurt, right?* Caritas shared with me a poem she wrote about Annie being able to walk again. She told me she had shared it with her church in Gisenyi on Annie Walking Day:

Let's Share Hope

If I had not known Annie's parent, I would not have
    known her,
Her parent being filled with mercy and love,
He is grieved when seeing people in trouble and strives
    to help them.

I did not meet Annie, but people told me about her,
Those who saw her,
Celestin and Simon Pierre, told me about her happiness,
About her gladness and hospitality.
She ignored her disability.

I did not meet her, but I did see her,
In the picture, in the hospital bed after undergoing surgery,
Even during that time, she never stopped laughing,
Her smile means a lot to me.
I did not meet her, I saw her in the family picture,
Smiling so nicely.

I did not meet her, but on reading her writing
I knew that Annie was full of hope,
That one day she would come out of her wheelchair
and then walk with her own feet.
After I had known her I discovered what was inside her,
I determined to walk with her,
Wherever I am, wherever I go,
Whatever I do, Annie is always with me.

Your picture is always kept close to me,
So every time I think of you, I look at it,
Reminding me that I'm with you and you with me.
I pray for you whenever I look at your picture.
Let us, we who share the same faith, come together with
    our different cultures,
Our church fellowship prays hard for that beloved.
Let's hope that the time is drawing near for her,
To be able to stand up and walk.

There is nothing impossible with God,
Because he has proved that over and over again.

When I first started traveling to Africa, my goal was to
give—whether education, mentoring, encouragement, prayer,

or partnership in various compassionate ministry projects. I never imagined how important my African friends' ministry to me would become as my family and I journeyed through the valley of the shadow of despair. Through their prayers, emails, acts of love, and visits to our home in the United States, our dear friends in Rwanda, Democratic Republic of Congo, and Ghana have sustained us through many, many trying times when we experienced far more doubt than hope. Like the friends who brought the man on a stretcher to Jesus in Mark 2, they brought us to Jesus when we were powerless to bring ourselves.

Two years after Caritas's Annie Walking Day, Caritas and Simon Pierre stayed with us in Colorado, where Caritas and Annie met for the first time. I'll never forget Caritas's eyes as she watched Annie take a few steps. It truly was a miracle and a celebration of the healing power of the body of Christ. Caritas's visit opened Shelly's and my tear-filled eyes to the miracle of Annie walking.

Now more than a decade after Caritas's Annie Walking Day, it is almost overwhelming for me as I consider our friends in Africa—especially those struggling with HIV/AIDS, hunger, and few opportunities for education or jobs—and how they have loved us. They have been Jesus to us. They've been a cruciform community, making real the resurrection of Christ in ways we didn't know we needed but never could have persevered without. Our friendship continues with Simon Pierre and Caritas to this day. They are no longer friends but family now. Whenever I talk with them, they never fail to ask about Annie.

Annie has been walking unassisted for more than ten years now. She won't ever run a marathon, but she can do the walking she needs to do. She recently had another surgery to remove what the doctor called "impressive" bone fragments from her elbow. Some days are better than others for Annie, since she never has a day when she is completely without pain. Life has turned out far better for her than Shelly or I ever imagined twenty years ago. But it's still not easy. I don't believe in happily ever after. What I do believe is that somehow, someway, in ways I can never fully fathom, God does indeed "do immeasurably more than all we ask or imagine, according to his power that is at work within us" (Ephesians 3:20). And God most often does that through authentic Christian community.

Our African sisters and brothers in Christ have been and continue to be the eyes, ears, hands, feet, and voice of Christ to us. In ways I can never fully explain, their love and prayers held us fast during a time when I was empty of faith and full of doubts. Caring Christian community has sustained my family and me throughout our journey with Annie's bone disease. At its best, Christian community is a means of grace. We help one another see God in our midst when we're too overwhelmed with grief, circumstances, disappointment, or doubt. When we need him the most and expect it the least, the resurrected Jesus meets up with us and walks the dusty, doubt-filled road of life with us, hand in hand.

How Can We Manage Doubt's Impact?

I do not have any formulas or happily-ever-after thoughts for managing doubt in the life of faith. Rather than overcoming doubt, I believe we need to befriend it as a normal and necessary part of a growing faith in Christ. Doubt is indeed a difficult and sometimes fickle friend and teacher. But doubt is also an essential part of a life fully lived for Christ. Here are some of the practices that have been important for me in developing a more resilient faith in the face of doubt.

- Be transparent with God about doubt. Pray the Psalms. Lament. Pray the Lord's Prayer.
- Worship regularly in a local church. Singing, praying, reading Scripture, hearing the Word preached, and being with loving sisters and brothers in Christ all bolster our faith.

- Be gentle with yourself. We all doubt in one way, shape, or form. You are not the first or the last to have doubted.

- Seek out a small group at church or school where you can be your true self. Such a group needs to be safe and offer confidentiality. Speaking your doubts aloud to others will reduce their hold on you.

- Serve the vulnerable. If you do, you will receive far more than you give.

- I ask myself when in a season or moment of doubt: *Am I doubting the true God or a too-small god of my own invention?* Or, *Am I confusing the God and Father of our Lord Jesus Christ with some of the things I see the church doing in Jesus's name that bear little resemblance to the life Jesus lived or taught?*

- Befriending your doubts will drain them of much of their poison and control.

- Be patient with your doubts and questions. Few of life's deepest questions will be resolved in our lifetime. It's likely we will always have some questions and doubts about our faith because it's impossible to separate faith and doubt. They mysteriously require each other. And we are finite creatures, only dimly grasping the mystery of faith (see 1 Corinthians 13:12).

- Become familiar with the stories of those who have experienced doubt and deep suffering and how they remained faithful to God in spite of it. Here I think especially of those who were imprisoned in Nazi concentration camps yet maintained vibrant faith in the worst circumstances imaginable: Corrie ten Boom, Dietrich Bonhoeffer, and Etty Hillesum.

- Read books that expand your horizon of faith, especially those that help you better understand the reliability of Scripture and the historicity of the resurrection.

- Listen to podcasts. There are innumerable podcasts available that will bolster your faith in dark times.[21]
- Reflect on the lives of those who have positively influenced your journey of faith. These can be people you know or have met personally, but they don't have to be.
- Find mentors who challenge you to expand and deepen your walk with Christ. When we begin to ask lots of questions, struggle, and doubt, it's clear we need new teachers in our life. We will need to rise to the challenge of thinking more, not less, thinking deeper, not shallower.

Perhaps it's time to consider reading some of the authors who have helped me to more comfortably embrace the mysteries of faith: C. S. Lewis, Fyodor Dostoyevsky, Albert Camus, Flannery O'Connor, N. T. Wright, Dallas Willard, Anne Lamott, Wendell Berry, Mary Oliver, Viktor Frankl, Henri Nouwen, Eugene Peterson, and Thomas Merton. A thriving, honest faith is worth whatever intellectual pain it may cost us. Consider praying the well-known prayer of Thomas Merton that I have often prayed during times of doubt or dismay:

My Lord God, I have no idea where I am going. I do not see the road ahead of me. I cannot know for certain where it will end. Nor do I really know myself, and the fact that I think I am following your will does not mean that I am actually doing so. But I believe that my desire to please you does in fact please you. And I hope that I have that desire in all that I am doing. I hope I will never do anything apart from that desire. And I know that if I do this you will lead me by the right road though I may know nothing about it. Therefore will I trust you always, though I may seem to be lost and in the shadow of

---

21. See especially "Everything Happens" with Kate Bowler. From the podcast website: "Life isn't always bright and shiny, as Kate Bowler knows. Kate is a young mother, writer and professor who, at age 35, was suddenly diagnosed with Stage IV cancer. In, warm, insightful, often funny conversations, Kate talks with people about what they've learned in dark times." katebowler.com/everything-happens.

death. I will not fear, for you are ever with me, and you will never leave me to face my perils alone.[22]

FOR REFLECTION

- Who is in your life with whom you can be vulnerable about questions and doubts?
- Find a group of friends with whom you can share your doubts and who will support you in prayer and check up on you from time to time.
- If you could write a letter to yourself about your doubts and questions, what would you write?
- Like those who brought the man on the stretcher to Jesus in Mark 2, who in your life has brought you to Jesus when you have been powerless to do it on your own?
- What would it mean for you to embrace doubt as a companion on the road of faith?
- Where do you need to up your game of reading authors who challenge, expand, and encourage your faith in new ways?

22. Thomas Merton, *Choosing to Love the World: On Contemplation* (Louisville, CO: Sounds True Publishing, 2008), 51.

4

PRISONERS OF HOPE

Developing Emotional Resilience

RESILIENCE TIP

Resilient people learn to live their lives with robust Christian hope so they can be emotionally resilient through the setbacks and storms of life.

> *Midway on our life's journey, I found myself in dark woods, the right road lost. To tell about those woods is hard—so tangled and rough and savage that thinking of it now, I feel the old fear stirring: death is hardly more bitter. And yet, to treat the good I found there as well. I'll tell you what I saw . . .*
>
> —*Dante Alighieri,* Inferno

The beauty of Scripture is that it is fierce with the sometimes harsh realities of life. It narrates warts and all human experience. It engages the heights and depths, joys and sorrows, despair and hopes, strengths and weaknesses, successes and failures of us all. It tells life like it is, not as we want it to be. When life threatens to overwhelm, it's comforting to know we are not the first ones ever to have walked through the valley of the shadow of death, crying out, "My God, my God, why have you forsaken me?" or pleaded with God to take away our thorn in the flesh.

To be human includes the possibility of depression—even deep, unrelenting depression.

The deepest truth of our lives is not despair, however, but hope. We are first and foremost people of hope—"prisoners of hope," as the prophet Zechariah puts it (9:12). If we are going to be imprisoned somewhere, I can't think of a better place than hope! As the theologian of hope, Jürgen Moltmann says, "Christian hope is the power of resurrection [within] life's failures and defeats." He says hope "quickens in us . . . courage for living . . . so that we can get up again from our failures, disappointments, and defeats and begin life afresh."[1] Hope is like having a lifeboat in stormy waters. Hope is the fuel for resilient living that keeps us going in the midst of despair.

None of us live problem-free, pain-free lives. "All God's children got problems," as it's been said. In order to finish our lives well, to keep the keel of our lives intact, we need hope, something that becomes especially true during times of depression. Not all of us will experience debilitating, clinical depression. But each of us at one time or another will know or love someone who does. Clergy members are not exempt. In fact, members of the clergy suffer depression at almost double the rate of the general population.[2] The unique, unrelenting stresses that clergy face as well as lack of healthy self-care contribute to this startling statistic. As expert in clergy well-being Arch Hart notes, "For many ministers, surviving the ministry is a matter of surviving depression."[3]

---

1. Jürgen Moltmann, *In the End—the Beginning: The Life of Hope*, trans. Margaret Kohl, (Minneapolis: Fortress Press, 2004), ix, xi.

2. Rae Jean Proeschold-Bell, Andrew Miles, Matthew Toth, Christopher Adams, Bruce W. Smith, and David Toole, "Using Effort-Reward Imbalance Theory to Understand High Rates of Depression and Anxiety among Clergy, *The Journal of Primary Prevention* 34 (2013): 439–53, https://doi.org/10.1007/s10935-013-0321-4; see also Mya Jaradat, "Religious Leaders Struggle with Burnout, depression and Anxiety—Just Like the Rest of America," *Deseret News*, May 2022, https://www.deseret.com/faith/2022/5/11/23058739/religious-leaders-struggle-with-burnout-depression-and-anxiety-pastor-mental-health-worker-shortage.

3. Archibald D. Hart, *Coping with Depression in the Ministry and Other Helping Professions* (Nashville: Word Publishing, 1984). If you are clergy, I strongly encourage

Scripture and Depression

In almost no other area of life is it more important to learn what Scripture says about being fully human than in the area of depression. Perhaps surprisingly, we find that biblical heroes of faith were no strangers to depression. I say "surprisingly" because, whenever I preach a sermon on depression or talk about it with students, most are surprised at the number of examples from Scripture of those who experienced something like what we call depression today. Here are a few examples:

- Cain became angry and felt dejected over God's acceptance of Abel's sacrifice and not his own (Genesis 4:5).
- A demoralized and exhausted Elijah asked God to take his life (1 Kings 19:4).
- Multiple times Jonah despaired and asked God to let him die (Jonah 4:3, 8, 9).
- King Saul suffered from some kind of mental illness that was only calmed by music (1 Samuel 16:14, 23).
- If you've read the psalms, you'll know that David was no stranger to emotional torment (Psalm 6:6; 22:14–15; 69:1–3, 20).

There are many psalms that speak of the experience of depression. In Psalm 13 David starts out feeling God-forsaken, but by the end of the psalm we find him praising God. In the course of six verses, David's emotional dislocation is resolved. If only things worked that quickly in real life, right? It's likely that what may have been a long depression was telescoped into a few verses. If this is the case, how long did David wrestle with his dark feelings—months, years, perhaps an entire lifetime?

---

you to take a look at the Duke Clergy Health Initiative resources for self-care and well-being found at https://divinity.duke.edu/initiatives/clergy-health-initiative/learning.

Psalm 88 is another depression psalm that is attributed to the Korahites rather than to David. In contrast to Psalm 13, this psalm starts depressed and overwhelmed and ends in the pit of despair with the words "darkness is my closest friend." Unlike Psalm 13, there is no positive resolution. The darkness lingers, hanging thickly in the air as we move on to Psalm 89. Or perhaps we stay in Psalm 88 for a while and live in its shadow because it feels like home to us during a particularly trying season of life.

When we read the Bible through the lens of depression, we will see several other scriptures that speak of depressive experiences as well:

- Jeremiah became so discouraged with his prophetic ministry that he cursed the day he was born (Jeremiah 20:14).

- The apostle Paul was so brutally harassed by detractors emotionally and physically that he at times "despaired of life itself." (2 Corinthians 1:8).

- In the garden of Gethsemane, the disciples fell asleep, "exhausted from sorrow" (Luke 22:45).

- Even Jesus cried out in despair: "My soul is overwhelmed with sorrow to the point of death" (Matthew 26:38). With the words of Psalm 22 he also lamented from the cross, "My God, my God, why have you forsaken me?" (Matthew 27:46; Mark 15:34). Whatever Jesus was going through at that moment, we know that, as fully God and fully human, he was experiencing the depths of human emotion along with us. It's deeply comforting to know the God of the universe understands and even shares our pain.

I love that Scripture is realistic and vulnerable about the heights and depths of human emotion. It gives us hope that—since we are not the only ones ever to experience depression—we too can recover and rediscover hope, energy, and our purpose for living.

My Story

As I mentioned in the introduction, I went through a deep depression after I had been a lead pastor for five years. I later learned that my experience is not uncommon among pastors. Coming out of seminary, I was idealistic. I thought that if a church wasn't growing numerically, it was failing. I believed that my calling as a pastor was to achieve, accomplish, and get results. There were only two options for me: succeed or fail. There wasn't much room for the mystery of God or the messiness of life in my theology. My theology at the time led to an either/or, yes-or-no, this-or-that kind of faith. As I look back at my thirty-two-year-old self, I can see clearly the coming disaster.

In the early years of my ministry in Colorado, I did not sleep adequately, eat healthily, or exercise regularly.[4] I also did not manage chronic stress well, or my unrealistic pastoral expectations. All of this created an extreme vulnerability to depression. Slowly, I began to find myself discouraged not just one day a week but every day of the week. I felt my energy levels dropping. I couldn't get enough sleep. I always felt tired. I began to lose motivation. When I pressed on the accelerator of my life to get moving, nothing happened. There was no more fuel in the tank. I had never heard about the relationship between burnout and depression. I had no idea what was happening to me.

I struggled alone for many months. I did not know I was experiencing clinical depression. I knew I wasn't myself, but I didn't know how to label it. I didn't have the language or experience to describe it. A doctoral class I took with Dr. Arch Hart at Fuller Seminary finally opened my eyes to what I was going through. Oddly enough, as soon as I had the language to describe my feelings, I quickly descended fully into the dregs of depression. The deeper I slid into the pit of despair, the more ashamed I became.

---

4. I talk about my struggles in these areas in *Healthy. Happy. Holy: 7 Practices toward a Holistic Life*.

I hid my feelings from my wife and my church. I couldn't bear to admit my depression to Shelly because I believed she had married me because I was strong, an achiever, and would one day be a "successful" pastor. Our kids were preschool age at the time. I'd get up with Shelly in the mornings during the week, help get the kids dressed and fed, and then Shelly would take them to daycare and go to work. As soon as they were out the door, I'd go back to bed and sleep until noon.

I believed depression was the end of my ministry. There were many days I feared I would not make it—in ministry or life. I could not imagine ever experiencing joy or excitement again. I felt like I was walking around in a weight suit. Each step, every movement, took an enormous amount of energy. The pain was nearly intolerable from morning until night. The pain felt physical but also went even deeper than that, into the very depths of my soul. I even considered taking my own life during the worst of it. I've asked myself many times since, *Why do some people take their own lives while others get better?* I don't know. I wish I did.

I've heard too many times after someone has taken their own life: "How could they have been so selfish?" I can tell you from personal experience that it's not selfishness. When someone is so mentally ill that they are experiencing excruciating, unrelenting pain, taking their own life feels like the only sensible thing to do to make it stop. It's one of those things that—unless you have experienced it yourself or been close to someone who has—is nearly impossible to imagine. Those who take their own life because of depression are deeply ill. Depression needs to be treated as the illness it is. Christians should not spiritualize it or shame those who suffer from it. By "spiritualizing" depression I mean reducing the cause of depression to spiritual factors alone, such as shallow faith, lack of commitment to Christ, not praying or reading the Bible enough, or other "quick fixes" that some Christians think are the solution—while ignoring the very real neurochemical, biological, and psychological causes.

This season of life was also a difficult time for our marriage. Shelly and I had always been best friends and our marriage full of fun and adventure. But now I was withdrawn and depressed. Professionally we were at very different places. At the time, her career in hospital administration was taking off, and I felt like all my years of preparation for ministry were being flushed down the toilet. Our kids were young. It would've been an exhausting season even for someone who was not depressed. Shelly and I both wondered, *Is this as good as it gets?*

Eventually, I came to the place where I felt like it was time to admit my depression to my church. I'll never forget the Sunday I told them about the depression that had been slowly suffocating me for several months. I thought my ministry there was over. I believed my church had hired me to be capable and energetic. No church wanted a depressed pastor. I felt ashamed. I felt worthless. I felt like a failure. I was also terrified. Admitting my depression to my church was one of the hardest things I have ever done. After the service was over, I went to my usual place near the door to greet people as they left. My stomach was tied up in knots as I feared the worst. I expected to hear a litany of rejection and watch people unable to look me in the eye as they ran out the door, never to return. Instead, what I heard from person after person was some form of, "Pastor, that was one of your best sermons! I've been on antidepressant medication for years. It's helped me so much. I couldn't function without it."

I was dumbfounded. I had no idea how many people in my own church had either been or were still depressed or suffered from some other kind of mental illness. I had never received such reactions to any sermon I had preached before. I learned that morning that my church had just been waiting for me to admit I was human—just like them. I discovered they longed to have a pastor who walked alongside them. They needed a pastor who was able to identify with their pain and struggle rather than one who stood on a pedestal of perfection. Miraculously, at this moment my true ministry started. They began to view me as one of them. I was now a wounded healer,[5] walking alongside them rather than running up ahead, dragging them along.

Medication and Mental Illness

I was fortunate that my depression was largely circumstantial, brought on due to my unrealistic ministry expectations and mistaken ideas about God. After I painstakingly worked on these areas of my life with the help of a counselor and spiritual director and read many books on mental health, I was able to go safely off medication after a couple years. But this is not the case for everyone. I have several family members and dear friends who need to be on medication for depression, anxiety, or bipolar disorder for the rest of their lives. There is no shame in taking medication for any form of mental illness. Humans are complex beings comprising spirit, body, mind, and emotions. Depression and other mental illnesses cannot be prayed away any more than a broken leg. Certainly, prayer helps in many ways both seen and unseen, but no one has ever re-grown a lost limb from fervent prayer. God has created us in such a way that the spiritual, physical, mental, and emotional aspects of our lives are entangled in a holistic union of soul. Christlike holiness is the healing and renewal of our entire self in Christ.

There are many versions of depression. Some are a result of external factors like chronic stress, illness, criticism, loss, a broken relationship, or perceived failure. Others stem from family-of-origin patterns, trauma, abuse, genetics, gender identity or sexual orientation, or unhealthy brain chemistry. Of course, our brain chemistry can be impacted by any or all of the other items. This is why we need to take the body seriously in our relationship with God. The incarnation tells us just how important the body

---

5. See Nouwen, *The Wounded Healer: Ministry in Contemporary Society* (New York: Image Books, 1979).

is to God. God himself took on a human body, experiencing the same things we do. Even Jesus had increased levels of cortisol and lowered levels of serotonin after a long day of ministry. One of the many beautiful things God desires is to heal us "through and through . . . whole spirit, soul and body" (1 Thessalonians 5:23). When we live a life of Christlike holiness, we focus not only on the spiritual aspects of our lives but also on the well-being of our bodies by developing regular (not perfect) habits of physical and mental health.

Maybe you've been taught to think that taking medication for mental illness is a sign of weakness. If that's the case, I want to point out that medication for mental illness is a means of grace. It is one of God's gracious means to heal and restore us to health. Medication for any kind of illness can be a means of grace every bit as important as worship, prayer, or Communion. The body and the spirit are both important to God. God is working for the redemption of our whole lives, including our bodies. The Wesleyan doctrine of prevenient grace affirms that God works through science to give human beings wisdom to treat cancer, chronic pain, viruses, heart problems, and many other life-threatening conditions. It's not an either/or between God and science; it's that God works through every area of humankind to bring about "the life that is truly life" (1 Timothy 6:19). If you find it difficult to keep taking your medication, perhaps it will be helpful for you to think of it as a gift from a loving God who wants the very best for you. Medication is one of the many wonderful ways God heals and restores us to fullness of life.

You may have noticed, but we in the church don't always like to talk about mental illness. As I've shared my story of depression in various contexts over the years, I've gotten the impression that the church would rather talk about sex than depression—and just think how much we like to talk about sex in the church, right? Depression is one of those topics we'd rather ignore because it doesn't lend itself to easy answers. I like simple solutions as much as the next person, but this is not the way life often works.

Instead of there being a specific formula to overcoming mental illness, we often experience more ambiguity than certainty. A mature Christian life is one that learns to embrace uncertainty and mystery, as we saw in chapter 3. The truth of our lives is that life is hard. Humans are fragile. And God will never quit loving us no matter what. Those of us who are afflicted with mental illness can indeed lead lives of joy, delight, gratitude, and hope like anyone else. We may just have to work harder at it sometimes.

Depression as a Severe Mercy

Depression was a "severe mercy" in my life.[6] What I mean by that is that I don't want to ever go through the heartache of depression again, but I'm so thankful I *did* go through it because I will be forever changed as a result of what I learned from it. Alexander Solzhenitsyn, a Russian dissident during the time of communism in the former Soviet Union, once said of his experience in the Russian Gulag: "Thank you, prison, for having been in my life." That's the way I feel about depression. *Thank you, depression, for having been in my life.* I can't imagine who or where I'd be today if I had never gone through deep depression. God used depression to transform my life for the better. Notice I said that God *used* it—not *caused* it. Depression was both the worst and the best thing I've ever gone through. C. S. Lewis's words ring true in my experience: "Pain insists on being attended to. God whispers to us in our pleasures, speaks in our conscience, but shouts to us in our pains: it is his megaphone to rouse a deaf world."[7]

---

6. This poignant phrase comes from Sheldon Vanauken, *A Severe Mercy* (New York: HarperCollins, 1977).

7. C. S. Lewis, *The Problem of Pain: Human Suffering Raises Almost Intolerable Intellectual Problems* (New York: Macmillan, 1962), 93.

God does not cause depression any more than God causes illness or other forms of suffering. But God uses the raw materials of pain to create beauty and to strengthen the broken places in us—similar to the Japanese art of *kintsugi*.[8] *Kintsugi* is an ancient art form of repairing broken pieces of pottery.[9] Broken ceramic pieces are reassembled to create new pottery that becomes even more beautiful and valuable than the original unbroken vessel. We hear echoes of this in the apostle Paul's words that our lives "are like clay jars" (2 Corinthians 4:7, CEV). We are cracked pots through which the light of Christ shines. Leonard Cohen beautifully wrote of this in his song "Anthem": "Ring the bells that still can ring/Forget your perfect offering/There is a crack, a crack in everything/That's how the light gets in."[10] And I would add, that's how the Light shines out.

At the heart of *kintsugi* is the creation of beauty from brokenness. As Makoto Fujimura says, "Kintsugi does not just 'fix' or repair a broken vessel; rather, the technique makes the broken pottery even more beautiful than the original."[11] That's exactly what God does for those of us who have been deeply wounded by depression or other forms of mental illness. God promises to give the Jewish exiles in Isaiah 61 and to those of us suffering from mental illness "a crown of beauty instead of ashes, the oil of joy instead of mourning, and a garment of praise instead of a spirit of despair" (v. 3). God will indeed create something beautiful out of the deep ugliness of depression. Corrie ten Boom testifies of her firsthand experience of the utter faithfulness of God even in a Nazi concentration camp: "There is no pit so deep that [God] is not deeper still."[12]

---

8. Rev. Raquel Pereira from Portugal was the first one to teach me about *kintsugi*.

9. For a wonderful description of the process and art form of *kintsugi*, see Makoto Fujimora, *Art and Faith: A Theology of Making* (New Haven, CT: Yale University Press, 2020), 43ff.

10. Leonard Cohen, "Anthem," *The Future* (1992).

11. Fujimora, *Art and Faith*, 44.

12. Corrie ten Boom, *The Hiding Place* (Old Tappan, NJ: Fleming H. Revell Company, 1971), 217.

Unexpected Gifts of Depression

I have experienced many unexpected gifts from depression. Because I went through depression, I'm a more loving, kind, compassionate, and empathetic person than I used to be. I still have a long way to go, but depression worked open-soul surgery in me in a way no other experience in my life ever has. As painful as depression was and as hopeless as I felt for what seemed like endless years, I would not trade what I learned or how I grew during that time for anything. That said, it's important to mention that there are those for whom depression never completely leaves, who feel weighed down by it daily. These sisters and brothers find little of redemptive value in depression or mental illness. Experiences like theirs keep me from offering false comforts or uttering promises of happily ever after. Life is too messy and unpredictable to do so in good faith.

Challenging emotions, like depression, anger, frustration, or doubt, can arouse the energy needed to pray earnestly, ask others for help, or search for creative responses to our circumstances (*can*, though such responses are not guaranteed). Depression provoked me into becoming a more resilient person. Over time it helped me be a better preacher and more caring pastor. I had to hurt badly enough from depression that I had no other choice but to become open to examining the toxic thoughts and expectations I had for God and life that kept feeding my depression. Concentration camp survivor Viktor Frankl's wise words ring deeply true in my experience: "When we are no longer able to change a situation . . . we are challenged to change ourselves."[13] Depression forced me to reconsider the distorted ways of thinking that were making me sick.

---

13. Frankl, *Man's Search for Meaning*, 112. If you have not read this book of profound wisdom born in the midst of the fires of Auschwitz, I encourage you to put it on your reading list.

Distorted Thoughts

One of the most important discoveries I made during my recovery from burnout and depression is that my depressed feelings were largely due to negative and pessimistic thinking. This discovery helped me begin to read the Bible through a different lens. Verses like Romans 12:2 became life-giving to me: "Don't be like the people of this world, but let God change the way you think. Then you will know how to do everything that is good and pleasing to him" (CEV). Philippians 4:8 was also pivotal: "Finally, brothers and sisters, whatever is true, whatever is noble, whatever is right, whatever is pure, whatever is lovely, whatever is admirable—if anything is excellent or praiseworthy—think about such things." Paul's emphases on the transformation of the mind and to keep thinking about the good, the true, and the beautiful helped me to learn to think in more positive ways and slowly begin to feel more hopeful.

Of all the things I learned in the midst of depression, the most valuable insight I received about the emotional life is this: *If we change the way we think, we change the way we feel, perceive, and act. Our thoughts create our feelings and our feelings provide the motivation and perspective from which we act.*[14] William Backus, a pastor and counselor, describes this process succinctly: "What is crucial in our lives is not what happens to us but how we *interpret* or understand what happens to us; not what others do but how we *explain* what they do; not what is but what we *believe* about what is."[15] It is not the circumstances of life that cause our emotions but our thoughts or interpretations of those circumstances

---

14. This is when I began to make connections between spiritual formation and psychology that I had never seen before. Rather than seeing faith and psychology as opposed, I began to see how the psychological field of cognitive behavior therapy (CBT) echoed many scriptural ideas. See the National Institute of Health's description of the history and main ideas behind CBT at https://www.ncbi.nlm.nih.gov/books/NBK470241.

15. William Backus, *Learning to Tell Myself the Truth* (Minneapolis: Bethany House Publishers, 1994), 77.

that lead to our feelings. Sad or blue feelings can be an accurate reflection of what is taking place in our environment, but many times they are a result of misinterpreting people and life events or even misunderstanding God's character and the way God works in our lives. This is where irrational, unrealistic, or false beliefs, rather than truthful interpretations of what is actually taking place, can undermine our feelings and mental well-being.

Ten Cognitive Distortions

There are at least ten cognitive distortions that feed into depressed feelings. The following list has been helpful for me in identifying the negative thoughts that kept kindling my depression. See how many of these distorted ways of thinking you identify with.[16]

1. All-or-Nothing Thinking

This mode of thought sees life in all-or-nothing, either/or terms, but life is rarely only one way or the other. Such a mentality ignores the fact that most of life is more like the volume control on a stereo than an on/off switch.

2. Overgeneralization

The temptation here is to take an isolated event and make a broad generalization about the rest of life from it. This happens when we think that, because we have failed in one area of life, we're a failure in every area. We may fail a math test, for example. This does not mean we are a failure as a math student, let alone a failure as an overall student. It was just one test on a particular day. Tomorrow is a new day.

---

16. In this section I have drawn from and summarized the thoughts of Backus, *Learning to Tell Myself the Truth*, 70–76; David Burns, *Feeling Good: The New Mood Therapy* (New York: William Morrow, 1980), 32–43; and Siang-Yang Tan and John Ortberg, *Understanding Depression* (Grand Rapids: Baker Books, 1995), 78–79.

3. Mental Filter

Here our life lens fixates on the negative events in our lives while ignoring the many other good things going on. In other words, we focus on the challenges of life instead of seeing that there are also many positive things taking place at the same time. What happens is we filter out the good and fixate on the negative. Recall Paul's admonition to keep thinking about "whatever is true, whatever is noble, whatever is right, whatever is pure, whatever is lovely, whatever is admirable . . . excellent or praiseworthy."

4. Disqualifying the Positive

People may pay you a compliment, but you do not hear them. You may discount positive comments or experiences by attributing them to luck or lack of insight. You may think, *If people really knew what I am like, they would not say such nice things to me.* As David Burns says, "If you constantly throw cold water on the good things that happen, no wonder life seems damp and chilly to you!"[17] As my mother has always reminded me: *If someone pays you a compliment, say thank you.*

5. Jumping to Conclusions

This is automatically assuming that something is the case without clear evidence to support the conclusion. Two examples of this cognitive distortion are:

a) Mind Reading

Here we assume we know the thoughts and intentions of others. Let's say someone behaves in a certain way toward you, so you assume that person does not like you. You are so convinced of your conclusion that you do not bother to find out if it is true. Your assumption of their feelings then drives how you behave

---

17. Burns, *Feeling Good*, 35.

toward them in the future. Or think of calling or texting someone but not hearing back from them in what you consider a timely matter. How do you interpret their lack of response? Do you tell yourself, *I know she received my message. Does she not care? She must be mad at me.* Or do you say to yourself, *Something must have come up. She has been under a lot of pressure lately. She's probably distracted. She will call me back when she is able.* It's all too easy to project our insecurities onto someone else in instances like these. Changing the stories we tell ourselves is crucial to growing a healthier emotional life.

b) The Fortune Teller Error—Crystal Ball Gazing

Here we live as if we have a crystal ball that foretells only misfortune. We predict the future before it ever arrives. This is the classic idea of borrowing trouble from tomorrow. Jesus, of course, wisely tells us not to do that (see Matthew 6:34). I think of the Palantír Stone in *The Lord of the Rings* series. Anyone who possessed one of these "seeing stones" was inevitably brought under control of the dark lord Sauron, and was only allowed to see worst-case scenarios in the future. Despair was one of Sauron's most powerful allies.

This kind of distortion was one of the most powerful temptations for Shelly and me in the early years of Annie's bone disease. We could only see heartbreak in her future. Because of our fear, we were unable to imagine a brighter future for her. When we crystal ball gaze, fear and despair become our dominant emotions.

6. Magnification (Catastrophizing) or Minimization (Dismissing)

This is what can be called the binoculars trick. We either magnify negative experiences or minimize positive experiences, depending on which way we have the binoculars turned. A sure recipe for depression is to habitually exaggerate our setbacks and minimize our self-worth. Think of Numbers 13, where twelve leaders of Israel were sent to explore the promised land and report back to Moses what they found: "We seemed like grasshoppers in our own eyes, and we looked the same to them" (v. 33).

7. *Emotional Reasoning*

In this distorted way of thinking, emotions are taken as fact. If we feel a certain way, we believe it to be true rather than questioning or debating the accuracy of our emotions. We need to recall that feelings are not infallible guides to truth. The truth about ourselves and our circumstances is found in God, not in our emotions.

8. *"Should" Statements*

This happens when we focus on the "should" or "ought-tos" of life rather than considering the actual situation we are facing. We can become so rigid in the way we live our lives that we end up "shoulding" all over ourselves. Examples of this might be telling ourselves any of the following: *I should not be depressed. I should be happy. I should not be so lazy. In order to be accepted, I should please others.* It also needs to be pointed out that "should" statements are not always wrong, particularly when such statements "reflect ethical demands that may bring about guilt that is both appropriate and potentially helpful. (It would have been a good thing if Adolf Hitler had experienced guilt for his behavior.)"[18]

9. *Labeling and Mislabeling*

Here we describe our mistakes with sentences beginning, "I am a . . ."

Suppose we make an honest mistake. It's one thing to think, *Oh, I made a mistake. I need to be more careful the next time so I don't make the same mistake."* It's a completely different thing to say to ourselves, *I am a failure.* None of us can be defined by a

---

18. Tan and Ortberg, *Understanding Depression*, 79.

single label. Our lives are too complex and dynamic to be frozen in such a way. The grace of God affirms that we are always much more than even our worst mistakes.

10. Personalization

This is feeling personally responsible for a negative event or outcome that is not primarily our fault. As an example, a pastor could think something like, *Our church is not growing. If I were a more prayerful pastor and a more effective leader, our church would be growing. It's my fault things are not going better.* There are many things that go into the growth of a church. If there were easy formulas to follow, every church would grow!

It is my hope that learning to recognize these ten forms of distorted thinking can help you identify irrational thought processes that may be causing you mental or emotional harm. As you identify these patterns of thought and use Scripture to defeat them, you will find your emotional life taking on a much more hopeful and joyful hue.

Learned Helplessness

There has been a lot of psychological research in the last fifty years that supports the words of Paul from Romans 12 and Philippians 4. Much of this research has been done by a psychologist named Martin Seligman and his associates at the University of Pennsylvania.[19] Seligman and his associates did a series of experiments that demonstrate it's possible to learn to be hopeful or hopeless. Neither hopefulness nor helplessness is a given; both are learned attitudes. It is especially important to recall this as we

---

19. The following includes summaries and paraphrases of Seligman's description of these experiments. See Martin E. P. Seligman, *Learned Optimism: How to Change Your Mind and Your Life* (New York: Pocket Books, 1990), 19–30.

consider how we can grow in our ability to manage depression and become more emotionally resilient.

Seligman's experiments in helplessness and hopefulness involved dogs. Please remember that we've come a long way in the last few decades regarding the appropriate treatment of animals in any kind of experiment. How Seligman and his associates treated dogs in this experiment would not be considered morally acceptable today. The dogs in the experiment were put in cages where they received small electric shocks. One set of dogs was put in a cage with a button that, if pushed, immediately stopped the shocks. These dogs quickly learned to push the button and stop the shocks. Another group of dogs were put in a cage where there was nothing they could do to stop the shocks, which occurred at random intervals. The dogs in this cage eventually quit jumping around and cowered in the corner even when they weren't being shocked. We might conclude that, because they felt hopeless to change their circumstances, they learned to be helpless.

In the second phase of the experiment, they put all the dogs into a new type of cage where there were two compartments separated by a low wall. All the dogs had to do to stop the shocks was jump over the barrier. Those that had earlier learned to push the button to stop the shocks learned quickly that jumping over the barrier would do the same. But the dogs that had previously learned that nothing stopped the shocks—this group did not even attempt to cross the barrier. Once the shocks began, they lay down and whimpered. Even though relief was a simple jump away, they didn't move. They gave up. It was like they had come to believe that their actions made no difference. It's as if they were saying to themselves, *Why should I move? I'm going to get shocked no matter what, so why try to avoid it?* We could categorize this response as a type of Eeyore syndrome—a way of defeatist thinking that produces a sense of helplessness that leads to hopelessness.

The reaction of the hopeless dogs has come to be known in the psychological world as "learned helplessness." Happily, the helpless dogs were eventually taught how to avoid the shocks, which is perhaps one of the most important outcomes of these experiments—that formerly helpless dogs could be taught to become hopeful. One of the many important implications of these experiments for humans is that if dogs could be "immunized" against learned helplessness by learning self-agency, then so can humans.

As much as I do not condone the methodology of the experiments performed on the dogs in this study, the results of the study have been crucial for me in learning how to manage depression and develop new strategies for living in the hope of the gospel. Underneath the helpless dogs' failure to be resilient was the loss of hope that their actions mattered. That loss of hope led them to quit trying. We find that this same sequence is at work in the minds of those suffering from depression as well. As the writer of Proverbs observed, "Hope deferred makes the heart sick, but a longing fulfilled is a tree of life" (13:12). The key difference between hopeful and hopeless people is how they understand and explain the failures, setbacks, criticism, or negative events of life.

Seligman and his colleagues went on to do research into what kind of people are most likely to lose hope. They found very different thought patterns between people who are hopeful and those who are hopeless. The key to these differences is the explanatory styles we use to explain failures, setbacks, or criticisms. What enables some people to persevere in the midst of hardship while others give up at the first sign of difficulty? According to Seligman, our habits of hopelessness or helplessness determine whether we will persevere or give up.[20] Our explanatory styles are most often habits of thought learned in childhood and adolescence, but they can also be learned and become more deeply embedded throughout adulthood. Even Christians are not immune to helpless explanatory

---

20. Seligman, *Learned Optimism*, 43.

styles, which is why it's so important that we learn the habit of living in the hope of the gospel. To view our lives through the good news of Christ crucified and resurrected is one of the most effective antidotes to depression. Of course, as we've discussed already, knowing and loving Christ does not automatically prevent mental illness from taking hold. Some who live full lives in the gospel do so with the help of medication—and that's okay.

There are three dimensions to a negative explanatory style: permanent, pervasive, and personal. Hopeless people lean toward an explanation of their troubles that is *permanent.* They believe there is nothing they can do to change their circumstances. This was largely how I felt about my life and ministry when I began to spiral into depression. The second explanatory style expressed by those who have learned to be helpless is *pervasive.* Those who engage in this explanatory style may think that one setback undermines everything else in life. Negative thoughts tend to compound on each other, leading to a downward spiral. The third explanatory style is *personal.* Whatever the problem or failure is, it must stem from some personal deficiency.

I started reading about Seligman's research while writing my doctoral dissertation. It didn't take long to discover that his conclusions regarding permanence, pervasiveness, and personalization described my depression all too well. I felt that my circumstances would never change, that I was a failure in every area of my life, and that I alone was the cause of all my problems. It was next to impossible to feel hopeful with these kinds of thoughts swirling around. As I reflected with a counselor, it became clear that such pessimistic self-talk had been my habitual way of viewing myself and my circumstances from my earliest memories. It filled me with hope to consider that, just as I had learned to think in pessimistic ways, I could slowly begin to shift my thoughts about God, myself, and my circumstances in a more hopeful direction. Hope that a new day would eventually dawn slowly began to seep into my life.

Paul: Model of Resilience

The apostle Paul was an amazingly resilient person. His response to his circumstances deeply encouraged me during my season of depression. His vulnerability about the many challenges, setbacks, hardships, and suffering he experienced while spreading the gospel throughout the first-century world offers us a model for how to live a more emotionally resilient life. Paul faced injustice, imprisonment, accident/disaster, beatings, sleepless nights, hunger, and even death. In Corinth there were "super-apostles" who severely criticized him and even preached to discredit him (2 Corinthians 11:5; 12:11). There was also Paul's thorn in the flesh that constantly dogged him (2 Corinthians 12:7). We don't know what specifically the thorn was, but it appears to have been a chronic illness or injury that caused deep pain.

Yet because of the resurrection power of Christ living in him (Philippians 3:10), he was able to keep running the race God had marked out for him even in the midst of many obstacles (1 Corinthians 9:24–27). The keel of Paul's life was deeply anchored in Christ: "We are like clay jars in which this treasure is stored. The real power comes from God and not from us. We often suffer, but we are never crushed. Even when we don't know what to do, we never give up. In times of trouble, God is with us, and when we are knocked down, we get up again" (2 Corinthians 4:7–9, CEV).

Paul experienced just about every obstacle human beings can face, yet he learned to live in the hope of the gospel in such a way that, even though he was knocked down many times, he got up one more time than he was knocked down. The hope of Christ and the energy of the resurrection kept him going in the midst of adversity. The apostle Paul is someone who has learned to live, think, and persevere in the hope of the gospel.

It's fascinating to consider how Seligman's explanatory styles worked themselves out in Paul's life and ministry.[21] Paul's life is a

---

21. I first heard some of the following ideas from a sermon by John Ortberg.

living example of how we can train ourselves to live in the hope of the good news of Christ. Rather than Paul saying, "My problems are permanent," he says instead, "Christ is eternal." The conclusion that Paul came to was that his problems were temporary since Christ was eternal: "For our light and momentary troubles are achieving for us an eternal glory that far outweighs them all" (2 Corinthians 4:17). He's saying, *My problems may be tough, painful, even overwhelming at the moment, but they will not last forever. I have God's promise on that. God is at work. God is with me. Christ is permanent; therefore my problems are temporary.* It's hard to imagine how Paul could have described his troubles as "light," but his deeply christological perspective enabled him to make such an audacious statement.

Christ for Paul was also universal. It was impossible for him to go anywhere that Christ was not already present. This theological conviction gave Paul the confidence to endure sailing in storms, suffering, and many other hardships. Paul was confident that Christ was universal and pervasive—not his problems. This is prevenient grace: the pervasive presence of the Trinity always goes ahead of us and is always present to strengthen us wherever we find ourselves. Because Christ is everywhere, my problems are limited, Paul says. In the same way, our problems may be deeply painful and we feel despair pulling us down, yet Paul says that in light of Christ our problems are never permanent or pervasive. Instead, they are temporary and limited. Therefore, we can persevere even if we walk with a limp like Jacob (Genesis 32:31).

"In Christ" is a unique phrase used by Paul 164 times in the New Testament. It's easy to skip over it as we read through Paul's letters, but the theological and personal implications of these two words are immense. *Because Christ is in me and I am in Christ, I am not alone. Because Christ is in me, he is comforting me. Because Christ is in me, he is transforming me into his image every day. Because Christ is in me, his strength is at work in me. Because Christ is in me, the problems that currently feel overwhelming will not have the last word. Because Christ is in me, nothing will ever be able to separate me from the love of God. Because the resurrection power of Christ is in me, the depression or anxiety I'm facing will not last forever.* Through prayer, medical intervention, counseling, and learning to live in the hope of Christ, each of us can develop habits of hope and serenity. We have hope because we are able to affirm that no matter the circumstances of our lives, God will indeed fulfill God's purposes in our lives (Philippians 1:6).

"In Christ" also has important ramifications for how we think about and relate to our neighbor. Because Christ is in me, he is also my neighbor. This means Christ is particularly present in the vulnerable, marginalized, and forgotten. Mother Teresa referred to the encounters we have with those experiencing hunger, thirst, exclusion, nakedness, illness, and imprisonment as Jesus in his most distressing disguise (see Matthew 25:31–46). Jesus himself said of this radical understanding of his presence, "Whatever you did for one of the least of these brothers and sisters of mine, you did for me" (Matthew 25:40). These two words, "in Christ," have tremendous implications for how we think about our ordinary lives, our adversities, and our neighbors near and far.

Strategies for Managing Depression

Before I bring this chapter to a close, I want to highlight several brief strategies and reminders for managing depression.

- If you are experiencing suicidal thoughts, please seek immediate help. United States residents who don't know of any local resources can call the Suicide and Crisis Lifeline by dialing 988 or visiting 988lifeline.org. (If you are counseling someone who is experiencing suicidal thoughts in the U.S., call the Suicide and Crisis Lifeline at 988 for them and wait until they have received the help they need. Another option is to drive them to a local emergency room and stay with them until someone else can join them.)

- See a licensed counselor. Even if you're on medication, I firmly believe in counseling alongside medication. Counseling, among many things, helps us understand the sources of our depression or anxiety and can provide helpful strategies for managing mental illness. If you can't find the energy to make an appointment—which was the case for me for several months—consider asking a loved one to make an appointment for you.

- If your condition requires medication, please view it as a means of grace. Medication of any kind is God's gracious gift to restore us to fullness of life.

- Please know you are far from the only Christian ever to experience depression. Depression is the common cold of the emotions. Far more experience it than we would dare to imagine.

- Sabbath rest, managing stress, engaging in play and hobbies, regular exercise, adequate sleep, healthy eating habits, and life-giving relationships are all crucial to emotional well-being. My book *Happy. Healthy. Holy.* might be helpful here.

- I find it life-giving to regularly ask myself: *What is breathing life into me? What is bringing me joy? What is sustaining me?* If I can't answer these questions, then I need to look at how to boost joy in my life or consider that I may be falling into depression and need to make an appointment with a mental health professional.

- Examine your thought life. Of all the things I learned in the midst of depression, the most valuable insight I received about the emotional life is this: *If we change the way we think, we change the way we feel, perceive, and act.* Our thoughts create our feelings, and our feelings provide the motivation and perspective from which we act.

- Learn to tell a different story. Is the story you are telling yourself about God's activity in your life faithful to the story Scripture tells from Genesis to Revelation about the character and purpose of God? Is the story you are telling yourself the only possible story? Have you considered all the facts? Are your problems truly permanent, pervasive, and personal, or does the resurrection story of Christ put your life and your neighbor's life into a radically new and hopeful light?

- An important strategy when we feel depressed or anxious is to hit the pause button on our thought process to identify the thoughts going through our mind. As William Backus says, "You feel the way you think; you think the way you believe. . . . Where our thoughts lead, our emotions will surely follow."[22] Thoughts create feelings. With God's help and a little practice, we can tweak our thoughts to create a more hopeful outlook. Memorizing Scripture is a crucial resource for learning to counter and exorcise long-held distorted ways of thinking. Committing various scriptures to memory will transform our lives by the renewing of our minds (see Romans 12:2).

- Spending time in creation has been an essential practice for me when I feel blue, anxious, or overwhelmed. Sensing the love of God circulating throughout creation breathes life, brings joy, and sustains me on dark days. Wendell Berry testifies to the medicine of creation in his own life:

When despair for the world grows in me and I wake in the night at the least sound in fear of what my life and my children's lives may be, I go and lie down where the wood drake rests in his beauty on the water, and the great heron feeds. I come into the peace of wild things who do not tax their lives with forethought of grief. I come into the presence of still water. And I feel above me the day-blind stars waiting with their light. For a time I rest in the grace of the world, and am free.[23]

22. Backus, *Learning to Tell Myself the Truth*, 15.
23. Berry, "The Peace of Wild Things," *The Selected Poems of Wendell Berry* (Washington, DC: Counterpoint Press, 1988), 30.

As helpful as these strategies can be, please remember that they require willingness to set out in a new direction. God provides the power for us to change.

Closing Prayer

Loving God, thank you for being with us in the midst of the storms, setbacks, and failures of life. I pray for all those who carry the heavy burden of depression or anxiety. May you give them courage to reach out for help, the strength to persevere, and the hope that their current nightmare is temporary. May you give them the assurance that, even though the despair of Good Friday weighs heavily upon them right now, the bright hope of Easter Sunday is already dawning. In Jesus's beautiful name, amen.

FOR REFLECTION

- Have you ever struggled with depression? After reading this chapter, can you identify the primary causes of your depression?
- What did you learn from this chapter about depression that you did not know before? How will this knowledge help you in your ministry of self-care and your ministry to others?
- What theological, medical, and psychological insights about the emotional life did you gain from reading this chapter? How do these insights challenge or provoke the way you have looked at the emotional life in the past?
- With which stories, examples, or strategies do you most identify with and why?

5

LOVE NEVER FAILS

Living a Life That Matters

RESILIENCE TIP

Resilient people learn to live the Christian life as a way of faithful love rather than a pursuit of success.

> *So, friends, every day do something that won't compute. Love the Lord. Love the world. Work for nothing. Take all you have and give it to the poor. Love someone who does not deserve it. . . . Plant sequoias. . . . Put your faith in the two inches of humus that will build under the trees every thousand years. . . . Laugh. Laughter is immeasurable. Be joyful though you have considered all the facts. . . . Practice resurrection.*
> —Wendell Berry, "Manifesto: The Mad Farmer Liberation Front"

> *Don't aim at success—the more you aim at it and make it a target, the more you are going to miss it. For success, like happiness, cannot be pursued; it must ensue, and it only does so as the unintended side effect of one's personal dedication to a cause greater than oneself or as the byproduct of one's surrender to a person other than oneself. Happiness must happen, and the same holds for success: you have to let it happen by not caring about it. I want you to listen to what your conscience commands you to do and go on to carry it out to the best of your knowledge. Then you will live to see that in the long run—in*

the long run, I say—success will follow you precisely because you had forgotten to think of it.

—Viktor Frankl, Man's Search for Meaning

I took another walk around the neighborhood and realized that on this earth as it is—The race is not always to the swift, nor the battle to the strong, nor satisfaction to the wise, nor riches to the smart, nor grace to the learned. Sooner or later bad luck hits us all.

—Ecclesiastes 9:11 (MSG)

My vocation is love!

—Saint Thérèse of Lisieux, The Story of a Soul

God has placed within each of us the desire to live lives that matter. We want to make a difference in God's beloved world by comforting the pain of others, working to lessen injustice, showing love to the unloved, and serving the underserved. Any time we are involved in significant life change, whether in our own life or that of others, it takes time. We can't microwave character change. Wounds do not heal overnight. The trauma of communities in despair will take generations to transform. Any significant creative and redemptive kingdom-of-God work in the world will take far longer than any of us can imagine. So how do we know if we are "succeeding," or making progress? How do we remain faithful when we know the seeds God has given us to plant have been planted but nothing seems to be growing?

The world's cultural pressure to achieve, accomplish, and succeed is exhausting. Consumer culture has made an idol of success, and it is making many sick. At work we are pressured to pad the bottom line. Those in ministry experience high expectations to produce visible church growth. How do we navigate these turbulent waters? How do we separate who we are as a child of God from what we produce at work or in the local church? How do we remain resilient when life, work, or ministry do not produce visible results—when we don't make enough sales, don't get a promotion, or our church numerically declines despite our best efforts? How do we respond when life does not turn out the way we imagined? Resilient people persevere in the midst of hardship and apparent failure.

Many of the causes of stress, depression, and anxiety in our day are related to toxic theologies of success. I know many good Christians who think their lives are a failure because they once made a mistake, or their family failed to live up to certain ideals, or a particular dream never materialized, or they have labored in largely hidden and small places where the fruits of their labors are few and often invisible. This is why developing a healthy theology of success is crucial for learning how to be the kind of person who can remain resilient in the face of disappointment, setback, and failure.

You may not be accustomed to thinking about the importance of theology for daily life, but this is one of those places where our theology can make or break us. Whether laity or clergy, we desperately need a theology that can serve as a secure anchor for the bumps, bruises, disappointments, imperfections, and storms of life. This chapter will help you reimagine success in life and ministry in light of the biblical imagination of faithfulness and fruitfulness, rather than consumer culture's fixation on achievement and accomplishment.

In order for us to think biblically about success, it's important to ask good questions:

- What counts as success for a Christian?
- How do we know when we are successful?
- How are success and failure related?
- Is success a biblical word? Should Christians strive for success?
- What is failure?
- Is failure bad, or is it a necessary stage in growing into "the whole measure of the fullness of Christ" (Ephesians 4:13)?

- What other words or images can Christians use to describe what a life well lived looks like?

One way to begin to respond to these questions is to ask yet another: What does God value most? Fourteenth-century priest Thomas à Kempis cuts straight to the heart of the matter: "Without love good works are worthless, but with love they become wholly rewarding no matter how small and insignificant they may seem. Indeed, God places more importance on the reason you work than on how much work you actually do. A person does much who loves much."[1] À Kempis is clear: love is the final criterion by which our life will be measured. Love is what God values most.

Scripture calls into question the way our cultural empires define success. A biblical understanding of success has little to do with ability, achievement, and accomplishment and much more to do with love, faithfulness, and fruitfulness. As Paul put it: "The only thing that counts is faith expressing itself through love" (Galatians 5:6). He's saying that only the love God has for us and the love we have for God and share with others ultimately matters. Love is the biblical criterion of a Christian understanding of success. Keeping love at the center of our theology and life will revolutionize the way we think about success, the purpose of our lives, and what it means to live life well.

In the introduction to this book, I told the story of John Stephen Akhwari from Tanzania, who became injured while running the marathon in the 1968 Olympics. Because of his injuries, he finished last in the race. Conventional wisdom would call him a failure or a loser because he finished last. A kingdom-of-God perspective says he succeeded because he didn't give up but ran his race faithfully. The way he finished the marathon in the 1968 Olympics, despite excruciating pain from his injuries, provides us important clues for how to run

---

1. Thomas à Kempis, *The Imitation of Christ*, trans. William C. Creasy (Notre Dame: Ave Maria Press, 1989), 44.

our God-given races. God calls us to be faithful, to do the best we can with our particular gifts, abilities, and circumstances. God certainly does not want us to do our work half-heartedly. The important lesson here is that outcomes and results are God's business, not ours. Thomas Merton cautions us not to make an idol of results:

> Do not depend on the hope of results. When you are doing the sort of work you have taken on, essentially an apostolic work, you may have to face the fact that your work will be apparently worthless and even achieve no result at all, if not perhaps results opposite to what you expect. As you get used to this idea, you start more and more to concentrate not on the results but on the value, the rightness, the truth of the work itself.[2]

Stories of Faithfulness and Fruitfulness

The soil in which fruitfulness takes root and flourishes is faithfulness. Henri Nouwen's words strengthen my resolve toward faithfulness: "We have been called to be fruitful—not successful, not productive, not accomplished. Success comes from strength, stress, and human effort. Fruitfulness comes from vulnerability and the admission of our own weakness."[3] As the Lord Jesus told the apostle Paul: "'My grace is sufficient for you, for my power is made perfect in weakness'" (2 Corinthians 12:9). True biblical success is humble and modest and usually displayed more clearly in vulnerability and weakness than in invincibility and strength. For a similar approach to living as Christlike disciples in a way that is humble, modest, and even quotidian, see Joshua R. Sweeden and Nell M. Becker Sweeden's 2022 release from The Foundry Publishing, *Holiness in a Restless World*.

---

2. Merton, "February 21, 1966," *Thomas Merton: A Life in Letters*, ed. William H. Shannon and Christine M. Bochen (New York: HarperOne, 2008), 262.

3. Nouwen, "Called to Be Fruitful," *Plough: Another Life Is Possible* (September 21, 2016), https://www.plough.com/en/topics/faith/discipleship/called-to-be-fruitful.

What follows are stories of people I have known personally or read about. Each has tutored me in what it means to live a faithful, fruitful, appropriately vulnerable life. Perhaps you will recognize yourself or a loved one in these stories that reflect true biblical success and lives well lived. I trust these stories will affirm your faithfulness to God even in the midst of whatever hardship, chronic pain/illness, criticism, or seemingly few visible results you may be experiencing in your life.

Stacy Schoech

Stacy Schoech was born with an immune deficiency disease that led to chronic bouts of pneumonia and long-term lung damage. National Jewish Health, a nationally renowned hospital in Denver specializing in immunology and respiratory illness, was Stacy's second home. In the early years of my pastoral ministry in Colorado, I visited Stacy and her family a couple days a week in the hospital. Because of the time and experiences we shared together over the years, they became like family to me.

Stacy was our favorite babysitter. She babysat often for our son, Jimmie. By the time our daughter was born, however, Stacy was sick frequently enough that she only watched Annie a couple times. Stacy died on the morning of her thirtieth birthday, less than six months after Annie was born.

Stacy was not a success by worldly standards. She did not amass money, status, or degrees. Even though she didn't accomplish glamorous things with her life, she exemplifies a life lived faithfully and beautifully for Christ. Stacy's biggest success was that she was a healing presence to others despite chronic illness. Stacy was what Henri Nouwen calls a "wounded healer." She offered her wounds as a source of healing for others, even in the midst of her own overwhelming pain. How can a life be more beautiful than this?

Stacy was a conduit of God's healing to other people. It did not matter that Stacy's life was largely hidden from public view. Every person who encountered Stacy recognized the undercurrent of love in her life. Her love so overflowed to others that there were more than two hundred people at her funeral. Stacy's funeral was one of the most sad and joyful experiences in my life. It was a glimpse of heaven. As her pastor, I was privileged to be part of her homegoing. One of Stacy's most treasured possessions was a Precious Moments figurine that pictured an angel comforting a woman crying at the gates of heaven with the words on the bottom, "No Tears Past the Gate."

I have never experienced a more remarkable example of a wounded healer than my friend Stacy. Her faithfulness to God in the midst of illness and pain continues to mentor me. Her life speaks encouragement to me in the midst of my own dark moments. When I consider what a truly successful life looks like, I think of Stacy. Upon entering the gates of heaven I imagine Jesus's words resounding in such a way that everyone heard Stacy's welcome: "Well done, my good and faithful servant. My daughter, I loved you in life and will continue to love you throughout eternity." Stacy represents all who experience chronic illness yet faithfully serve God in small, often unnoticed ways.[4]

Shirley Poff

Perhaps you are a teacher and wonder if you're making a difference. I think of my fourth-grade teacher, Shirley Poff, who gave me a chance to do extra work and move up several reading levels. I started kindergarten when I was four and turned five shortly after. I started slowly in school. Even though my mom read to me all the time, I struggled to read by myself at grade level. As a result, I was placed in the "slow" reading group and didn't like school much until I was in Ms. Poff's fourth-grade class. I don't know why she took a special interest in me. It's possible she gave all the students in my class the same opportunity.

---

4. Stacy's family has graciously given me permission to share her story.

I'll never know. What I do know is that I flourished with her as my teacher.

Several years ago I found Ms. Poff's address and wrote her a long letter expressing my gratitude. She graciously wrote back. We've since exchanged many Christmas letters over the years. I will never cease thanking God for Ms. Poff. God only knows what my educational path might have been if it weren't for her. Without her belief in me, I might not have gone on to do well in school, graduate from college and seminary, earn a doctorate, or become a pastor or professor. Believe me, I was an obnoxious kid, easy to ignore. It would have been the easiest thing for an exhausted, underpaid teacher to think, *Why invest extra effort into Joe? He'll never amount to anything. Why bother?* But Shirley Poff saw something in me. Her confidence in me helped me believe in myself. My sense of self has never been the same since she dared to give me a chance to prove myself.

If you are a teacher, then God has put impressionable young girls and boys into your hands to love, encourage, nurture, and give opportunities. I imagine there are days and weeks you wonder if what you do is making any impression at all, let alone a lasting one. There are so many forces at work affecting the mental health of teachers these days: undeserved criticism by parents, student performance expectations, an overwhelming number of papers to grade, and little thanks or recognition of your faithful work. Thank you for what you do. It truly is making a world of difference, one child at a time. Hopefully it doesn't take more than twenty years for you to hear back from your students that the time and love you invested in them has made a difference in their lives.

An Unnamed Young Boy: The Feeding of the Five Thousand

"What's in your hand?" God asked Moses (see Exodus 4:2). Several hundred years later, an unnamed boy with a few dirty fish and dried loaves of bread gave Jesus what was in his hand. On a grassy Galilean hillside, the boy saw the large, hungry crowd that had gathered. He wanted to help, so he gave Jesus all the food he had brought with him: five crumbling barley loaves and two small fish. Barley loaves were the kind of bread eaten by the poorest of the poor. Even though the feeding of the five thousand is told in all four Gospels, only John says "small fish" (6:9). The boy, like Moses, gave God what was in his hand, however insignificant it may have seemed.

The disciples wanted to make the boy go away. "What's so little among so many?" they ask. In other words, "Lord, why bother? That's just a drop in the bucket. It's not going to make any difference." But when five dried loaves of bread and two small fish were given to Jesus in faith, they fed more than five thousand hungry men, women, and children. And there were twelve baskets of fish and bread leftover. In God's economy, much is made from little when it is put in God's hands.

Wangari Maathai

Perhaps you've never heard of Wangari Maathai, Nobel Peace Prize winner from Kenya.[5] She changed the world by planting trees to fight poverty and restore Kenya's forests. Planting trees was a service to her people, whose forests were being devastated and their streams polluted by the Kenyan government out of economic self-interest. Planting trees was her call from God even though it seemed small and insignificant.

When she was young, her brother persuaded their parents to send her to school. Few African parents sent their daughters to school in the 1940s. Maathai later received a scholarship to study in the United States and did doctoral work in Germany. She eventually felt called to go home to Kenya, where she earned a doctorate in veterinary anatomy from the University of Nairobi in 1971—the first East African woman to earn a PhD.

---

5. For her memoir see Wangari Maathai, *Unbowed: A Memoir* (New York: Anchor Books, 2007).

Her efforts to protect the land and the trees that had sustained her people for generations led her into direct conflict with the Kenyan government. Because she worked tirelessly for ecological justice, the Kenyan police sought to silence her by beating her a number of times, even bludgeoning her unconscious once. She was repeatedly jailed. Seven of her colleagues were murdered.

Maathai, a Christian, started small, planting seven trees in Nairobi. Five died, but two were still living at the time of her death in 2011. Her tireless efforts led to the planting of more than fifty million trees since she first began. She started the Greenbelt Movement and was awarded the Nobel Peace Prize in 2004. She said in an interview:

> We cannot solve all the problems we face: We are poor, we don't have water, we don't have energy, we don't have food, we don't have income, we're not able to send our children to school. There are too many problems we face. We have to break the cycle, and the way to break the cycle for us is to do something that is doable, to do something that is cheap, do something that is within our power, our capacity, our resources. Planting a tree was the best idea I had. . . . The tree for me became a wonderful way of breaking that cycle.[6]

She ended her interview by telling a story of a hummingbird that tries to put out a forest fire. When mocked by other animals, the hummingbird replies, "I'm doing what I can." I repeat these words often to myself when discouraged: *I'm doing what I can.*

Annie Gorman

If you read chapter 3, then you know something of the difficult journey of my daughter, Annie. So much of what I have learned about resilience has been because of Annie. She is one of the most resilient people I know. When Annie was a high school senior, she

---

6. Amitabh Pal, "Wangari Maathai," *The Progressive Magazine*, Vol. 69 No. 5 (May 2005).

started baking cupcakes to raise money for a medical clinic in rural Ghana. Her reasoning went something like this: *I can't change my bone disease. If I had been born in a developing country, I would have likely died a long time ago. But if I can save even one other kid from death, it will help me make some sense out of my disease.*[7]

Instead of two small fish and five crumbling loaves, Annie gave Jesus what was in her contracted, arthritic hands: the ability to make cupcakes. Because of her inspiration, more than $300,000 has been raised to build, equip, and connect the clinic to water and electricity. Her efforts led to four young women from the local community graduating from nursing school and serving at the clinic as registered nurses. Another local young woman and man trained as pharmacists and are also working at the clinic. Sixteen other young women are community health professionals, holding educational clinics and traveling throughout the villages surrounding the clinic, offering medical care to anyone who needs it.

More than ten years later, the clinic is touching hundreds of lives in the rural village of Namankwan in northeastern Ghana.[8] During one of the many times I have visited the clinic, I met with local tribal elders who spoke of the blessing the clinic has been to them and their community. They told me our partnership with them is reflected in a local proverb: *The lizard wishes to defend itself, but its front legs are too weak to fight for itself.* They said Annie had become their front legs. It truly took a village to build the clinic and educate its healthcare workers. Annie baked cupcakes. I advocated within my fields of influence. Many individuals and churches gave financial donations. And the local people of Namankwan built the clinic with their own hands.

All of it came about because of cupcakes. This is success in a different key. In a developing-world context without access to

---

7. See Joe and Annie Gorman, "Cupcakes and Compassion: Partnering to Build a Medical Clinic in Northeastern Ghana," *Nazarene Compassionate Ministry Magazine* (Spring 2013), www.ncm.org/assets/2013_issue_1.pdf.

8. If you try to locate Namankwan on Google Maps, the closest town is Garu.

advanced medical care, Annie likely would have died before her teenage years. There are many things she can't do because of her bone disease, but she tries to keep her focus on what she can do.

What's in your hand? What handful of stale bread and small fish has God put in your hand to serve the world in the name of Jesus? What's your tree to plant? What's your cupcake to bake? To which child can you offer love?

Pastors Who Serve in Season and Out of Season

There is the small-church pastor who is steady and faithful, in season and out of season (see 2 Timothy 4:2), whose church attendance declines or remains the same year in and year out. I've talked to many pastors who have seen so few visible results in their ministry that they feel like failures. Such pastors often suffer deep disappointment and chronic, low-grade depression. They love God and serve their churches faithfully in season and out of season. The faithful, small-church pastors I know and love demonstrate that pastoral success is never to be equated with numerical growth alone.

And what about the larger-church pastor whose self-worth is primarily wrapped up in church programs and numerical goals? I used to think it was only small-church pastors who struggled with inferiority complexes. As I've gotten to know pastors of larger churches over the years, I've discovered that many of them believe the only reason people love them is their position—not because of who they are as people. We often assume people in visible positions don't struggle. In reality, we all hurt in one way or another. This is one of the many reasons we must "Be kind, for everyone you meet is fighting a hard battle."[9]

---

9. This statement is often misattributed to Plato and Philo of Alexandria. It seems to have originated with John Watson, also known as Ian McLaren. Here is a link for more details on this quote's fascinating history: http://quoteinvestigator.com/2010/06/29/be-kind.

Tony Campolo's Childhood Church

More than seventy-five years ago a small Philadelphia congregation excitedly watched as three nine-year-old boys were baptized and joined the church. Just a few years later, unable to keep its doors open, the church sold its building and disbanded, an apparent failure. One of those three boys was Dr. Tony Campolo, prolific Christian author, professor emeritus of sociology at Eastern College, and one of the most influential evangelical Christian leaders of the latter half of the twentieth century. Campolo tells about his boyhood church:

> Years later when I was doing research in the archives of our denomination, I decided to look up the church report for the year of my baptism. There was my name, and Dick White's. Dick is now a missionary. Bert Newman, now a professor of theology at an African American seminary, was also there. Then I read the church report for my year: "It has not been a good year for our church. We have lost twenty-seven members. Three joined, and they were only children."[10]

As a former pastor of a small church, Campolo's story deeply resonates with me. Ministry in the local church is not only about the harvest we see today. We may plant, water, fertilize, and weed in faith for a crop we will never see. Even though there are few visible results, we trust that God makes things grow (1 Corinthians 3:7). This trust takes tremendous patience, even "the patience of Job."

You may feel that what you have to offer to God is too small, too insignificant, too feeble, or your circumstances too intractable. But Scripture constantly reminds us that our God is a liberating, empire-toppling, resurrecting God. Our God is a God

---

10. Marlene LeFever, *More Perfect Illustrations for Every Topic and Occasion*, compiled by the editors of PreachingToday.com (Wheaton, IL: Tyndale House Publishers, 2003), 317.

of broken-down shepherds, bungling disciples, mustard seeds, measly fish, stale bread, and a cross. These are unlikely ways for God to reconcile the world to himself. They are not the ways I would choose to save the world if I were God. Yet this is exactly the road on which the God and Father of our Lord Jesus Christ invites us to travel. The path of Christian discipleship is not about achievement, accomplishment, position, or prestige. It is faithfulness expressed in love. Faithfulness keeps loving and serving even when there are no outcomes. It keeps its eyes on God, not results. Faithfulness has to do with relationships rather than formulas, obedience rather than results.

It's hard to quantify faithfulness, especially for those involved in some form of ministry. What counts as success in God's eyes does not always make it onto the scorecards of those determining our livelihood. Hospital visits, prison visits, ministry to immigrant families, answering midnight calls, and staying with someone in the psychiatric ward until they are removed from suicide watch are faithful acts that may or may not give rise to visible results. And what about the faithful caregiver who lovingly cares for a chronically ill person day in and day out? Each of these acts expresses God's love for his precious lambs and builds the kingdom of God one person at a time.

A More Excellent Way

When we are led by a more excellent vision of the kingdom of God as "faith expressing itself in love" (Galatians 5:6), we will be less driven and distracted by the siren sounds of consumer culture's fixation on achieving, accomplishing, producing, and succeeding. There will be less exhaustion and more joy as a result.

Anjezë Gonxhe Bojaxhiu was led by the more excellent way of love. We know her as Mother Teresa. When she started saving one person at a time on the streets of Calcutta, she didn't do it to be noticed, to win the approval of others, to receive a Nobel

Prize, to have books written about her, or to have documentaries filmed of her work. She was simply obeying the call of God to serve "the least of these brothers and sisters" (Matthew 25:40), or what she often referred to as "Jesus in his most distressing disguise." Mother Teresa's theology of ministry was strongly influenced by her namesake, Saint Teresa of Avila, a sixteenth-century Spanish nun who wrote:

> The Lord does not look so much at the magnitude of anything we do as at the love with which we do it. If we accomplish what we can, his Majesty will see to it that we become able to do more each day. We must not begin by growing weary; but during the whole of this short life, which for any one of you may be shorter than you think, we must offer the Lord whatever interior and exterior sacrifice we are able to give him, and his Majesty will unite it with that which he offered to the Father for us upon the cross, so that it may have the value won for it by our will, even though our actions in themselves may be trivial.[11]

Note in particular Saint Teresa's words "the Lord does not look so much at the magnitude of anything we do as at the love with which we do it." When we view life through the theological lens of love, the pressure for us to make things happen on our own is removed. We are liberated to serve in whatever capacity God leads us. It may be small or insignificant. Or it may be visible and highly influential. Whatever our place of ministry, we trust along with Apollos and Paul that, even though we have been given the important responsibilities of planting, watering, and weeding, God is the one "who makes things grow" (1 Corinthians 3:7). Wherever we minister and in whatever capacity we serve, when we faithfully partner with what God is doing in the world, there

---

11. Teresa of Avila, *Interior Castle*, trans. E. Allison Peers (New York: Image Books, 1989), 233. Mother Teresa was also guided in her ministry by another namesake, Saint Therese of Lisieux (1873–1897), who was also known for doing small things with great love for God and others.

will be a harvest of faith, hope, and love all out of proportion to our efforts. Fruit follows faithfulness. This is a life well lived.

Fruitful Living

Living a life led by faithfulness rather than driven by success will look different in each of our lives. But one thing will be the same for us all: faithful living is a far less stressful way to live. It will create a more peaceful atmosphere for our family and friends. Our bodies, minds, and spirits will also thank us. We will be guided rather than driven. At the end of each day, we will be able to lay our weary heads on our pillows, confident that we have done what we can and leave the results to God. Like the parable of the growing seed, we trust that our best efforts are taking root, germinating, and producing a crop even as we rest (Mark 4:26–29). The only things that finally endure are God's love for us and our love for God, others, and all creation. As Richard B. Hays asserts, love is the biblical "criterion by which we should assess all that we do."[12]

My personal success creed is rather earthy and seemingly unspiritual. I like to think of it as thoroughly incarnational, however. It has little to do with effectiveness or success as they are commonly understood. A robust biblical theology of faithfulness reminds us that true success in life and ministry has little to do with achievements or promotions and everything to do with relationships and love. I pray by the grace of God that my life may reflect these beautiful words often attributed to Ralph Waldo Emerson. These words are really nothing more than a recasting of Paul's succinctly stated theological goal of the Christian life: "Do everything in love" (1 Corinthians 16:14):

To laugh often and love much; to win the respect of intelligent persons and the affection of children; to earn the appreciation of

---

12. Richard B. Hays, *First Corinthians, Interpretation: A Bible Commentary for Teaching and Preaching* (Louisville: John Knox Press, 1997), 232.

honest critics and endure the betrayal of false friends; to appreciate beauty; to find the best in others; to give of one's self; to leave the world a bit better, whether by a healthy child, a garden patch, or a redeemed social condition; to have played and laughed with enthusiasm and sung with exultation; to know even one life has breathed easier because you have lived—this is to have succeeded.[13]

You may be deeply disappointed by the way your life, family, work, or ministry has turned out. You had high hopes, but things have not turned out the way you imagined. Jesus experienced broken dreams as well. When he was crucified, his dream for the world seemed to be crucified along with him. The truth is that when his body was laid in the tomb, they were planting a seed in the ground. After the resurrection, as that seed erupted from the ground, it brought forth a harvest of previously unimaginable possibilities.

The Christian hope is that one day every wrong will be set right and every tear dried and all suffering redeemed. The resurrected Jesus says to us, *Keep hoping, keep praying, keep loving, keep serving, remain faithful, trust in God for the fruitfulness of your life and ministry. The seed is in the ground. God's harvest for you, your family, your ministry, and your church is just a matter of time.*[14]

The stories we tell ourselves nurture resilience and faithfulness. The late U.S. Congressman John Lewis was a passionate Christ follower, intimately involved with the Civil Rights Movement in the 1960s. He and Martin Luther King, Jr., were friends. Lewis, like King, was a fierce advocate for justice. His words give me hope and energy to stay in the struggle to remain faithful and resilient: "Do not get lost in a sea of despair. Be hopeful, be optimistic. Our struggle is not the struggle of a day, a week, a month, or a

---

13. According to the Ralph Waldo Emerson Society, this poem has been misattributed to Emerson. For a history of this popular inspirational poem, see http://emerson-legacy. tamu.edu/Ephemera/Success.html.

14. Some of these ideas were inspired by one of John Ortberg's sermons.

year, it is the struggle of a lifetime. Never, ever be afraid to make some noise and get in good trouble, necessary trouble."[15]

All of us will grow weary and be tempted to throw in the towel at some point. What will keep us going is the hope that what we do makes a difference, not only today but a difference that will outlast us all the way into God's fully consummated new creation. When I'm tempted to feel like my efforts to love and to change deeply entrenched systems of injustice make little difference, I open N. T. Wright's book *Surprised by Hope* and am encouraged to remain faithful:

> What you do in the Lord is not in vain. You are not oiling the wheels of a machine that's about to roll over a cliff. You are not restoring a great painting that's shortly going to be thrown on the fire. You are not planting roses in a garden that's about to be dug up for a building site. You are—strange though it may seem, almost as hard to believe as the resurrection itself—accomplishing something that will become in due course part of God's new world. Every act of love, gratitude, and kindness; every work of art or music inspired by the love of God and delight in the beauty of his creation; every minute spent teaching a severely [disabled] child to read or to walk; every act of care and nurture, of comfort and support, for one's fellow human beings and for that matter one's fellow nonhuman creatures; and of course every prayer, all Spirit-led teaching, every deed that spreads the gospel, builds up the church, embraces and embodies holiness rather than corruption, and makes the name of Jesus honored in the world—all of this will find its way, through the resurrecting power of God, into the new creation that God will one day make. That is the logic of the mission of God. God's recreation of this wonderful world, which began with the resurrection of Jesus and continues mysteriously as God's people live in the risen Christ and in the

---

15. John Lewis on Twitter (@repjohnlewis), June 27, 2018. For an outstanding book on Lewis's bold Christian faith and involvement in the Civil Rights Movement, see Jon Meacham, *His Truth Is Marching On: John Lewis and the Power of Hope*, (New York: Random House, 2020).

power of his Spirit, means that what we do in Christ and by the Spirit in the present is not wasted. It will last all the way into God's new world. In fact, it will be enhanced there.[16]

FOR REFLECTION

- What is your theology of success and a life well lived? You may want to set aside some time to reflect on what a life well lived looks like in the midst of the life you've been given to live. Then spend another period of time writing and revising it.

- What do you think? Is success a word that Christians should use to evaluate our lives? Or do you prefer more biblical words, such as faithfulness or fruitfulness? Why do you prefer one over the other?

- How have you been faithful to God, yourself, and those you love in spite of overwhelming and painful obstacles?

- What does faithfulness as a mother, father, husband, wife, grandparent, friend, brother, sister, son, or daughter look like to you?

- What does faithfulness as a pastor working with children, youth, or adults look like to you? As a chaplain or missionary? A lead pastor? A denominational leader? A stay-at-home parent? A college professor? A teacher? An employer or employee in your current work context?

---

16. N. T. Wright, *Surprised by Hope: Rethinking Heaven, the Resurrection, and the Mission of the Church* (New York: HarperOne, 2008), 208–09.

6

LOVE HURTS

Holding On through Suffering

RESILIENCE TIP

Resilient people learn to maintain hope in the midst of painful circumstances and in turn offer compassionate hope to others who are hurting.

> *God of compassion and love, we offer you all our suffering and pain. Give us strength to bear our weakness, healing even when there is no cure, peace in the midst of turmoil, and love to fill the spaces in our lives. Amen.*
>
> —*Service of Prayer for Healing,* Iona Abbey Worship Book

> *To the "why" of suffering we get no firm answer. Of course some suffering is easily seen to be the result of our sin: war, assault, poverty amidst plenty, the hurtful world. And maybe some is chastisement. But not all. The meaning of the remainder is not told us. It eludes us. Our net of meaning is too small.*
>
> —*Nicholas Wolterstorff,* Lament for a Son

> *The death of a beloved is an event that rings and rings through a life: bearing it is not a problem to be solved, but a long, slow piece of music to listen to. And mourning, like music, is best listened to with others.*
>
> —*Sara Miles,* Jesus Freak

I want to carry pain like a tree does, let the rings of my experiences push me to grow wider and stronger. I never want to forget each ring that holds everything I've witnessed, loved and lost. But I want to keep expanding.

—*Mari Andrew,* My Inner Sky

Our wounds are often an essential part of the fabric of our lives.
—*Henri Nouwen,* Life of the Beloved

Suffering comes uninvited into our lives. It takes many forms: depression, illness, chronic pain, loss of a job, death of a loved one, poverty, oppression, and more. Suffering knows our address. It hurts. It exhausts. It crushes. It crucifies. How can we remain resilient in the face of great pain? How can we comfort others in the midst of their pain?

My goal in this chapter is not to solve the problem of suffering but to help us think more clearly about how our theology sustains trust in God in the face of senseless suffering. I will also raise questions that I hope you will continue to reflect on and discuss, perhaps even with your church or small group. My intent is not to answer every question that has ever been raised in the face of pointless evil and pain but to help us think theologically about the presence of God among the suffering as well as consider our divine calling as the church to companion well in Jesus's name those who suffer.

The first time I experienced inexplicable suffering was when my father died. I was twenty-three. I was out of college, was serving as a full-time youth pastor, and had been married for under two years. Even though my father's death was sudden, he had been ill with schizophrenia for many years. He was an all-conference basketball player in high school, acted in the drama club, was very popular at school, and helped out on the family dairy farm. He enlisted in the Navy during the Korean war. His main job was decoding secret messages. During this time he contracted a virus that led to an extremely high temperature that some think may have created a vulnerability that led to his developing schizophrenia in his early twenties. I will never forget my grandmother's anguished words, repeated again and again, as I sat in the funeral home with her trying to pick out a casket: "A son is never supposed to die before his mother." His death has led me to wonder many times over the years, *Why did I live and my father die?* Because of my experiences of loss, I can never be a detached bystander when it comes to suffering. Suffering is not a puzzle to be solved. It has a face. It has a name. Perhaps it does for you as well.

Theodicy

Theology, as the study of God, helps us engage seriously the most vexing and personal questions of life, including, *Where is God when people suffer?* The attempt to answer such a question is called "theodicy" by philosophers and theologians and is usually presented as the age-old, familiar question, *Why do bad things happen to good people?* Theodicy comes from the Greek words *theos* ("God") and *dikē* ("justice"). Theodicy seeks to explain how the existence of a loving and sovereign God can be justified in a world where so many suffer for no apparent reason. Some theologians, like Stanley Hauerwas, question whether theodicy is a legitimate endeavor for Christian theology: "It is speculatively interesting to ask how the existence of a good and all-powerful God can be reconciled with the existence of evil in the world. . . . But when I confront the actual suffering and threatened death of my child—such speculative considerations grounding belief or unbelief seem hollow."[1] Like Hauerwas, I'm not a fan of the project of theodicy. Theodicy's attempt to explain why God and evil can coexist often strikes me as the exercise of an ivory-towered

---

1. Stanley Hauerwas, *Naming the Silences: God, Medicine, and the Problem of Suffering* (Grand Rapids: Eerdmans, 1990), 1.

theology that is disconnected from the actual sufferings of women, men, and children just like us. That said, I do find theodicy to be of value for considering how God is with us in the midst of inexplicable loss and pain. Let me explain what I mean.

Free Will

The free-will theodicy claims that much that we call evil may be explained through the misuse of human free will. Wars, accidents, poverty, ignorance, errors of human judgment, and sin account for much of human suffering—but not all of it. As an example from my state of Idaho, a mother was accidentally killed several years ago by her two-year-old son while they were shopping after Christmas. The mother had a concealed weapons permit, and when she turned her back for just a moment, the toddler reached into her purse, found the gun, and tragically shot and killed his mother.[2] This story continues to haunt me years later. Free will is a wonderful gift, but this is an example of a gift tragically gone wrong.

If our goal in such a tragedy is theodicy, we may speculate as to why God didn't prevent this horrible accident, but a pastoral-theological approach asks, *Where is God in such a situation?* A pastoral-theological perspective assures us that God is comforting the toddler, helping first responders bring order out of chaos, and begin a lifelong process of healing a traumatized family and community. One thing is clear, however: God did not cause this mother's death. The so-called free-will defense may help explain logically how such a heartbreaking accident may occur, but if we think it alone can make the absurd intelligible, we are asking it to do more than it can do.[3]

---

2. See Terrence McCoy, "The Inside Story of How an Idaho Toddler Shot His Mom at Wal-Mart," *Washington Post* (December 2014), https://www.washingtonpost.com/news/morning-mix/wp/2014/12/31/the-inside-story-of-how-an-idaho-toddler-shot-his-mom-at-wal-mart/.

3. Hauerwas, *Naming the Silences*, 73.

Natural Evil

We may also wonder about the origin of what are often called "natural" evils, such as viruses, tsunamis, earthquakes, tornados, hurricanes, and volcanoes. So-called natural evils are not necessarily evil, however, for there is a sense in which earthquakes and the like are thought to be part of an incredibly complex planetary system that makes possible the conditions necessary for the flourishing of life on earth.[4] Natural evils may also be seen as the groans of creation itself that reverberate between initial creation and creation's final consummation in a new heaven and new earth (see Romans 8:12; Revelation 21:1). Still others suggest that the persistence of natural evil is the result of a creation that is "wounded . . . in its uttermost depths . . . by a primordial catastrophe."[5] As helpful as these explanations of so-called natural evils may be for some, I do not find them personally or pastorally comforting when I think of my daughter's bone disease or friends or family who have children with genetic disorders.

What we need in the face of suffering is compassionate presence rather than theoretical explanation. As Nicholas Wolterstorff observes in the aftermath of his son's tragic death, "Instead of explaining our suffering, God shares it."[6] There is no definitive answer or completely satisfying solution as to why so-called natural evils persist. Rather than trying to provide an explanation for such evils, we will do well to remember that the purpose of Scripture is not to tell us why these things happen but to affirm God's presence with us and God's intent to one day redeem evil and suffering (Romans 8:28). Jesus used the tragedy of the tower in Siloam that fell and killed eighteen people not to provide an explanation but as a call to repentance and a reminder that life is

---

4. Thank you to my good friend Steve Smith, a geologist with the United States Geological Survey, who first suggested this idea to me many years ago.

5. David Bentley Hart, *The Doors of the Sea: Where Was God in the Tsunami?* (Grand Rapids: Eerdmans, 2005), 22, 62.

6. Wolterstorff, *Lament for a Son*, 81.

short and people should view the event as an impetus to repent rather than speculate (see Luke 13:1–5). In a similar way, God calls us to join hands with him in the alleviation of human suffering rather than speculating about its causes.

"Everything Happens for a Reason"

There's a folk theology that many gravitate toward when we hurt. We hear it often from the lips of those who themselves are not in pain but are trying to comfort those who are: *Everything happens for a reason.* The phrase sounds true and reasonable, doesn't it? It rolls off our lips so easily. We've even made a bumper sticker out of it. If God is all-powerful and all-loving, then there must be a specific and knowable reason for what we and our loved ones are going through, right?

While the sentiment behind this statement seeks to make sense of God's presence and sovereignty in the midst of suffering, the slogan itself actually expresses a toxic theology. When reasoned out fully, the theology behind this statement means that, if everything happens for a reason—i.e., is part of a meticulous, pre-determined divine plan—then God is responsible for everything that happens, including sin, evil, and suffering. Such a theology makes God the direct cause of illness, genetic disorders, earthquakes, tsunamis, and all other forms of suffering. In this view, God becomes the torturer and murderer of children and other innocents.

Ultimately, this view says everything is caused by God—joy and sorrow, happiness and pain—which works okay when everything is going well in life. But what about when things go wrong? If our operating system is based on a God who has a meticulous, detailed master plan, then God controls and causes absolutely everything. If everything in life is orchestrated according to a detailed divine blueprint, then when bad things happen we logically need to ask, *Why is God punishing me? Is God teaching me a lesson? What did I do to deserve this?*

You can see how confusing it gets. If God is doing every-thing, then it is difficult to figure out our role. And if God causes everything that takes place in our lives, it is difficult—if not impossible—to love a God who causes childhood leukemia. In this view of God, human beings are nothing more than puppets being manipulated by a puppetmaster. God is like the Wizard of Oz, who stands behind the curtain of our lives and pulls the levers and pushes the buttons that make everything happen. We are pawns in God's chess game.

You may be thinking, *Well, that's how I see it—God is control-ling everything.* But for me, this view totally breaks down when dealing with human suffering and tragedy. What about a parent who's just lost a child? Or someone who's been raped? Or a child who has been molested? Did God cause these evils to happen? A God who causes such things would be more like the devil than the God and Father of our Lord Jesus Christ.

A "divine blueprint" theology makes it difficult to love a God who visits pain and tragedy upon us and those we love. If we go down the road of "everything happens for a reason," then God is ultimately a monster. How can we possibly love—or trust—a God who causes illness and tragedy? This is why we must be careful in our theology, in the way we understand and talk about God. In this light it's understandable how some people become so disappointed with or angry at God that they find it hard to believe in, let alone love, God. If you genuinely thought God caused everything that happens, wouldn't you be disappointed with or angry at God? I would. And I have been. I was angry at God when I lived my life according to this toxic theology. But Scripture shows us a better way.

Jesus reveals to us a God who is loving, compassionate, just, merciful, and kind. Jesus is God with a human face. So, whenever we talk about why bad things happen, we must do so in light of who Jesus is. Jesus loved, cried with, and healed those who suffered. In light of the portrait of Jesus the Gospels paint, the "everything happens for a reason" theology that makes God more like the devil than like Jesus is inhumane and anything but Christlike.

Wesleyan theology rejects the idea that God predetermines everything ahead of time. Wesleyan theology understands God's power differently. Rather than hoarding power, Wesleyan theology believes that God shares power with us so we may partner with God in God's redemptive purposes.[7] God's power, according to Wesleyans, is most perfectly manifested not in a meticulous, predetermined divine blueprint but in Christ's vulnerable, suffering love on the cross. What we believe theologically about God's power has tremendous implications for how we in the church understand and respond to suffering. While we may submit to a God of absolute power and control, it is difficult to trust, let alone truly love, a God who treats us as puppets rather than beloved children.

Prevenient Grace

A Wesleyan theology of suffering also stresses that God's redemptive love is everywhere present. Because God's goodness indwells all creation, there is literally nowhere that God is not. This divine characteristic is commonly called *omnipresence*. Wesleyans often refer to it as *prevenient grace*. So where is God when unimaginable suffering and evil strike? Trinitarian theology affirms that the Trinity—Father, Son, and Holy Spirit—is with the abused, the trafficked, the sick, and the attacked to save, sustain, heal, and renew all things by God, in Christ, through the Spirit. Such divine loving presence "means that the Spirit was in Auschwitz's fiery pits of burning children, in the eye-melting heat of the Hiroshima blast—and most particularly, hanging on the cross of Jesus."[8] A robust Trinitarian theology helps us to see God in places our tear-stained eyes alone cannot see (Exodus 6:9; Luke 24:13–35; John. 20:11–16).

---

7. Michael Lodahl, *The Story of God: A Narrative Theology* (Kansas City, MO: Beacon Hill Press of Kansas City, 2008), 62.

8. Lodahl, *The Story of God*, 62.

Soul-Making

Another way Christians seek to make sense of evil and suffering is to speak of the good that can come from suffering (Romans 5:3–5). This is called "soul-making" theodicy. While growth in faith, hope, and love may develop as a result of faithful suffering, this ideology still does not explain *why* suffering occurs. Speaking in the wake of the mountain-climbing accident that led to the death of his son, Nicholas Wolterstorff writes:

> Suffering may do us good—may be a blessing, something to be thankful for. This I have learned. . . . How can we thank God for suffering's yield while asking for its removal? In the valley of suffering, despair and bitterness are brewed. But there also character is made. The valley of suffering is the vale of soul-making. How do I receive my suffering as blessing while repulsing the obscene thought that God jiggled the mountain to make *me* better?[9]

Wolterstorff's insights caution us to think carefully about what our theology of soul-making says about our understanding of God. To say that God allows rape in order to strengthen the soul of the victim makes God a sadist, for example. And who could possibly believe in a God who allows a child to be born with a terminal genetic disorder so the child can be an inspiration to others?[10] Even though unimagined good may come from suffering—and we must honestly acknowledge that sometimes it does not—this never makes extreme suffering "worth it." Cannot growth come through less painful and tragic means? There simply is no moral algorithm that can ever fully explain the loss of a loved one, let alone the suffering and death of millions.

---

9. Wolterstorff, *Lament for a Son*, 97.

10. In her poignant TED Talk, "I'm Not Your Inspiration, Thank You Very Much," Stella Young calls this "inspiration porn." http://www.ted.com/talks/stella_young_i_m_not_your_inspiration_thank_you_very_much?language=en.

The Limitations of Theodicy

Theodicy may seem like a reasonable enough pursuit when viewed from the outside looking in—that is, when it's undertaken at arm's length. I think this is one of the reasons many laypeople often shun theology in general. Too much theology reads and feels as if it's been conceived by someone who has little engagement with real-world realities, let alone acquaintance with the suffering of particular people.

Theoretical explanations for suffering are only satisfying to someone who's never suffered. When it's your suffering, endlessly seeking explanation often leads to bitterness rather than comfort. This was my experience in the wake of my pain after the death of my father. I read theology book after theology book expecting to find the definitive answer for why my father died at fifty and lived a drastically diminished life with schizophrenia for thirty years. The way theodicy is set up, it gives the impression that there *is* a final answer when there is not. It leads to endless, repeated questioning and even toxic doubt, which is not helpful, nor is it the approach of Scripture.

For pastoral-theological reasons, theoretical theodicies that explain the "why" of suffering are of limited value in a Christian theology of suffering. There simply is no logical formula that solves the problem of evil. While various theodicies have helped me better grasp some of the considerations involved in understanding why bad things happen to good people, I no longer find that theodicy alone satisfies. I don't so much want an explanation of why I suffer as I need a companioning presence with me *when* I suffer.

Jürgen Moltmann: Theologian of Hope

Jürgen Moltmann, known as the "theologian of hope," is one of the most significant theologians of the twentieth century. He and his childhood friends were conscripted into the German army at the age of seventeen. In 1943 he and his fellow troops were positioned to defend their hometown of Hamburg when Royal Air Force bombers dropped explosive and incendiary bombs that "kindled a storm of fire" that "burnt everything living and reduced every home to rubble."[11] More than forty thousand men, women, and children were killed in Hamburg during these horrible nights of bombing. Moltmann says of this experience, "For some inexplicable reason, the bomb which blew to pieces the school friend who stood beside me at the firing platform left me unscathed." He remained in the army another two years, during which he experienced "unending terror which destroyed the lives of millions."[12] Since Moltmann was not raised in a Christian home, theology and faith were remote realities. He shares about his experience:

> In that catastrophic night, for the first time in my life I cried out to God. "God, where are you?" That was my question in the face of death. It was not the theodicy question we are all familiar with—the question, how can God allow this to happen? That always seems to me like an onlooker's question. The person who is in the grip of a catastrophe, or is already in the jaws of a mass death, asks differently about God. And then came the other question, the one which has haunted me all my life ever since: why am I still alive and not dead like the rest?[13]

As a prisoner-of-war in England after the war, Moltmann received his first Bible from a chaplain. As he read through Psalms, he came across psalms of lament whose words "echoed what was in my own heart." When he read Jesus's anguished cry from the cross, "My God, my God, why have you forsaken me?" he "was

---

11. Moltmann, *In the End—the Beginning*, 33. Moltmann's story in this chapter is based on this book.

12. Moltmann, *In the End—the Beginning*, 33.

13. Moltmann, *In the End—the Beginning*, 34.

profoundly struck. I knew that this was someone who understands [me]. . . . That gave me the courage to live. I saw colours again, heard music again, and felt the stirrings of renewed vitality."[14]

During his years as a prisoner-of-war in England, the love that Scottish miners and English neighbors showed Moltmann and his fellow German prisoners helped restore their humanity. Their hospitality to him and his fellow prisoners-of-war "made it possible for us to live with the guilt of our own people, the catastrophes we had brought about and the long shadows of Auschwitz."[15] In this camp Moltmann was loved into faith in Christ. A young pastor and his wife, Frank and Nellie Baker, served a Methodist church near the camp. They often asked permission of the camp commander to bring a German soldier with them to church and eat Sunday dinner with them in their home. They shared God and their life with many prisoners during that time. One was Jürgen Moltmann, who said of their hospitality: "I want you to know that the seed of hope was planted in my heart around Frank and Nellie Baker's Sunday dinner table."[16] This was the beginning of the development of his theology of hope in the face of inexplicable evil and suffering. In the English prisoner-of-war camp, Moltmann began looking for the assurance that would give his life meaning and sustain him for the rest of his life. In a word, he was looking for hope—and he found it in the crucified, resurrecting one.

The moral authority of Jürgen Moltmann, who speaks of God's presence in the midst of unimaginable suffering, is undeniable. His theological career, stretched out over sixty years, has been a constant search to find a hope that can sustain him and others in situations of inexplicable suffering. His question is not, *God, why did you cause or allow this to happen?* But, *Where are you, God?* These are very different questions. The first is that of

---

14. Moltmann, *In the End—the Beginning*, 35.

15. Moltmann, *In the End—the Beginning*, 35.

16. Moltmann, *A Broad Place: An Autobiography* (Philadelphia: Fortress Press, 2009).

theodicy. The second is deeply theological, pointing to the God who promises never to leave or forsake us, even in the midst of the most horrific circumstances imaginable. This is what Moltmann calls "crucified hope."[17]

As Moltmann's story shows, we need the body of Christ to help us discern God's presence when we hurt. During the darkest times of my daughter's suffering, the church I pastored loved us. Our local church journeyed alongside us. Rather than trying to explain the why of Annie's suffering, they prayed for us, visited us at home and in the hospital, and brought meals to us. Their incarnational presence fostered hope when we were tempted to despair. They mourned and rejoiced with us (Romans 12:15). We sat together in the darkness of Good Friday. We rejoiced together at the empty tomb of Easter morning. We sang together songs of hope. We prayed together. We cried and lamented together. We celebrated weekly Communion together. We engaged in redemptive ministry to the suffering together.

The Church: A Community of Care for the Hurting

We are saved in hope (Romans 8:24). We yearn and lament[18] for a definitive answer to the problem of evil yet see only so far: "For now we see only a reflection, as in a mirror, but then we will see face to face. Now I know only in part; then I will know fully, even as I have been fully known" (1 Corinthians 13:12, NRSVUE). Even through what is often a "cloud of unknowing,"[19] we affirm that faith, hope, and love do indeed remain (1 Corinthians 13:13). The presence of the suffering/resurrecting one in the body

---

17. Moltmann, *In the End—the Beginning*, 48.

18. For an important resource on lament as a means of grace, especially in times of suffering, see Walter Brueggemann, *The Message of the Psalms* (Philadelphia: Fortress Press, 1985). See also Diane Leclerc, Brent Peterson, et. al., *The Back Side of the Cross: An Atonement Theology for the Abused and Abandoned* (Eugene, OR: Cascade Books, 2022).

19. See the spiritual classic written by an anonymous fourteenth-century English monk, *The Cloud of Unknowing* (San Francisco: HarperCollins, 2004).

of Christ sustains the Christian virtues of faith, hope, and love in the midst of senseless suffering. As Stanley Hauerwas affirms, "Historically speaking, Christians have not had a 'solution' to the problem of evil. Rather, they have had a community of care that has made it possible for them to absorb the destructive terror of evil that constantly threatens to destroy all human relations."[20] The church as a means of grace makes the unbearable bearable.

Churchly means of grace nurture faith, hope, and love as well as assure us of God's presence even when we suffer for no good reason. A biblical response to evil and suffering always looks and acts like the body of Christ.[21] A church that lives under the shadow of the cross and leans into the sunrise of the resurrection is the kind of community in which the suffering are welcome, pain is embraced, and companioning, incarnational presence is offered instead of easy answers and false comforts. Until the fullness of the kingdom comes, we labor in hope together for the day when God will raise up all who have suffered and "wipe every tear from their eyes. Death will be no more; mourning and crying and pain will be no more, for the first things have passed away" (Revelation 21:4, NRSVUE).

How to Respond to the Suffering of Others

When we are faced with the suffering of others, we often feel the need to say something to lessen the pain. Lack of adequate theological reflection can lead us to give careless and painful responses to those who suffer. We may not be aware of it, but our theology informs our response to those who hurt, verbally and in our actions. I will always be grateful that the church I pastored did not offer platitudes or even try to cheer us up. They simply

---

20. Hauerwas, *Naming the Silences*, 53.

21. Whenever I think of what the church is called to be, I think of the church where I was the lead pastor for almost twenty-one years. Even though I was the pastor, they shepherded my family and me during some of the most difficult times of our lives.

showed up. They visited us when we needed it and gave us space when we needed to be alone to grieve and process. They helped us to see that God was indeed with us through their concrete, loving actions. Their companioning love slowly healed our broken hearts and gave us hope to trust that a better day would eventually dawn.

A theology of suffering is incomplete without some specific pastoral resources for how to be with those who hurt. When someone is in physical or emotional pain, it is difficult to know what to do or say. It's a natural human response to want to fill the silence of suffering with words and explanations. As a result of our own discomfort, we feel the need to fill the silence with comforting words but too often find pious platitudes coming from our mouths. Our words are meant to reassure, but too often they injure the one who is already grieving. The following lists help us know how to respond more compassionately in times of grief. Not only will these help us to be more resilient, but they will also contribute to the resilience of the grieving. These are not exhaustive lists but are meant to help us be more intentional with the hurting.

Beware of Platitudes

Bumper-sticker theology tends to come out during times of grief and crisis. When we have not thoughtfully considered the theology and impact of our words, pious platitudes can come tumbling from our mouths rather than careful and compassionate theological responses. Because suffering "strips us of easy answers and false comforts,"[22] it's important that we do our best to refrain from saying the following:

- "I know how you feel." Death, suffering, and loss are unique. Our personal histories are unrepeatable and cannot be laid

---

22. Hauerwas, *Naming the Silences*, 30.

on top of one another like a template. Even if we have experienced a loss that seems similar on the surface, it is never exactly the same as someone else's. This moment in time is about the other person, not us. Our attempt to connect to the other person is laudable, but assuming that our pain is the same can be seen as insensitive and unloving. For example, even if you have been deeply depressed at some point in your life, it will be different in large and small ways from others similarly afflicted.

- "Everything happens for a reason." We've already discussed the harm of this toxic theological statement that points to a divine calculus that, if we only had access to it, would make sense of a particular loss. But the reality is, sometimes things just happen. Accidents happen. We get sick. Genetic abnormalities occur. There is not always a strict sense of cause and effect. Causes may remain hidden to us. The temptation to explain can be strong. The lack of clear answers and solid ground during times of loss can feel overwhelming. Kate Bowler says about this phrase, "The only thing worse than saying this is pretending that you know the reason. I've had hundreds of people tell me the reason for my cancer. Because of my sin. . . . Because of my aversion to Brussels sprouts. . . . When someone is drowning, the only thing worse than failing to throw them a life preserver is handing them a reason."[23]

- "Time heals." While the sharp edge of pain may dull over time, the sense of our loss may deepen. Recovery from grief takes as long as it takes. It's unique from person to person. We cannot hurry it. And we only make someone's grief worse if we tell them to hurry up or that they should be over their grief by now.

---

23. Kate Bowler, *Everything Happens for a Reason and Other Lies I've Loved*, 170. Bowler provides an even longer list than mine of things never to say to people experiencing horrible things. She also includes a list of helpful things to say and do for the hurting, born out of her own experience.

- "You are such an inspiration." This response has been called "inspiration porn." Those who live with disability or who suffer debilitating loss don't necessarily want to be an inspiration. They often struggle on a daily basis simply to survive. They don't feel like their efforts to survive are extraordinary. They are simply what is necessary to make it through the day. Again, the intent is noble, but it can come across as insensitive.

What NOT to Do When Caring for the Hurting

- *Don't compare someone else's pain with yours or someone you know.* In comparing pain, we usually mean well. We are trying to identify with the hurting. But pain is incomparable. Don't mention that you once had a cat run away so you know what it is to suffer. (Yes, I've heard this one before.) Instead, say something like: *I can't imagine what you're going through. Would you like to talk about it? Is there anything I can do to lighten your burden?*

- *Don't offer explanations.* For example, don't say, "Look at all the wonderful things you've been able to do in spite of your disability. All the pain you've experienced is worth it because of all the great things you've been able to do." My daughter says that if you do say something like this, you may get punched.

- *Don't give advice or try to fix it.* As Parker Palmer observes, "One of the hardest things we must do sometimes is be present to another person's pain without trying to fix it, to simply stand respectfully at the edge of that person's mystery and misery." Giving advice makes *us* feel better, not the other person. Palmer says there is an unspoken subtext: "If you take my advice, you may get well—and if you don't get well, I did the best I could. If you fail to take my advice, there's nothing more I can do."[24]

---

24. Parker J. Palmer, *Let Your Life Speak: Listening for the Voice of Vocation* (San Francisco: Jossey-Bass, 2000), 63.

Ministry to the hurting is always about the other person's needs. The time for our own therapy is when we meet with a counselor, not when we offer comfort to others.

- *Don't say the words "at least" to a hurting person.* You can imagine how hurtful it would be to say to a parent who has lost a child, "At least you have other children." Or to one who has lost their spouse, "At least you had so many wonderful years together." Equally insensitive are: *At least you will see them in heaven. At least you won't experience pain in heaven. At least they are no longer suffering.* What we need during such times is not an explanation, but loving, comforting presence. Kate Bowler says of "at least" statements, "Whoa. Hold up there. . . . At least it's not . . . what? Stage V cancer? Don't minimize."[25] While some "at least" statements may be true, they trivialize the person's grief, and they are hurtful rather than healing words. This is why we always need to ask ourselves before we speak, *Is this true, necessary, and kind?* All three need to be present in order to speak lovingly and compassionately in a time of loss. Come to think of it, these are important elements to consider before we say anything at all!

Things to Say

- *I don't know what to say. I'm so very sorry. I grieve along with you. My heart is broken too.* Nicholas Wolterstorff, who lost his twenty-five-year-old son in a mountaineering accident, says, "If you can't think of anything at all to say, just say, 'I can't think of anything to say. But I want you to know that we are with you in your grief.' Or even just embrace. Not even the best words can take away the pain."[26]

---

25. Bowler, *Everything Happens for a Reason and Other Lies I've Loved*, 169.
26. Wolterstorff, *Lament for a Son*, 34.

- *I weep along with you. I hold you in my heart wherever I go.* Don't be afraid to cry with the other person. Tears are compassionate. Tears heal. Jesus wept upon hearing of Lazarus's death. I once had a ministry student tell me, "I don't think I can ever officiate a funeral because I'd cry through the entire service." I responded, "If that happens, it would likely be the most powerfully pastoral act you could perform."

- *I'm praying for you.* It can be appropriate to tell someone we're praying for them, but we need to discern if this is helpful in each situation. We also want to be careful to show the fruit of our prayer in active love for the one who is hurting.

- *I loved them too. I miss them. I don't know how we are going to get along without them.*

- *I can't imagine what you're going through. My heart is broken.*

- *Would you mind telling me about your child? I want to know.*[27] You can adapt this to any situation by asking, "Would you tell me about . . . ? I want to know."

- We're often afraid to ask others to share with us about the loved one they have lost when in fact the thing they most want and need to do is talk about them. When it's appropriate, we can also say, "What were they like? How did you meet? What did they enjoy doing? What are some of your happiest and funniest memories of them?"

Things to Do

- *Offer comforting presence rather than explanation.* As we seek to be the eyes, ears, hands, and feet of Jesus to those who are hurting, one of the most healing acts we can offer is simply to be present, expressing unconditional love. It's likely that we will listen far more than we speak. We may need to

---

27. Samuel Wells and Marcia A. Owen, *Living without Enemies: Being Present in the Midst of Violence* (Downers Grove, IL: InterVarsity Press, 2011), 104.

listen the other person into speech. Our presence may mean cleaning the hurting one's house. Bringing a meal. Buying and delivering groceries, especially ice cream. Mowing their lawn. Taking out the garbage. Perhaps we don't need to say anything, but simply shed tears with them. Sometimes the other person can express these needs; other times we need to intuit what they need and just do it. During Parker Palmer's depression, his friend Bill asked for permission to come over to his house and give him a foot massage every afternoon. Palmer says, "He found the one place in my body where I could still experience feeling." Bill rarely spoke. When he did speak, it was to mirror Palmer's feelings back to him: "'I can sense your struggle today,' or, 'It feels like you are getting stronger.'" Palmer says, "I could not always respond, but his words were deeply helpful."[28]

- *Share appropriate touch.* As Samuel Wells and Marcia Owen observe, "The power of touch is an embodiment of the incarnation."[29] A genuine hug offered appropriately can be tremendously healing. I can't count the number of times I have held the grieving in my arms as they sobbed after the loss of a loved one. Even though I felt helpless in the moment, I was also aware that, because of the incarnation, my presence represented God's loving touch. In that moment, my embrace was God's embrace. I myself remember a hug given to me during a lonely time many years ago. I had been away from my young family for almost a month while teaching in Papua New Guinea. Naturally, I deeply missed them. I was at a missionary family's house one evening for dinner when another missionary from Australia gave me an unexpected hug I will never forget. It was not a little hug but a bear hug. And it lasted for close to ten seconds—which seems like forever when you're hugging a

28. Palmer, *Let Your Life Speak*, 63–64.
29. Wells and Owen, *Living Without Enemies*, 88.

stranger. It was not creepy in the slightest. I had not been hugged for almost a month and didn't know what to do as the other person embraced me. I finally relaxed in the embrace and realized I had no idea until that moment how much I missed and needed a hug. That hug was truly an embodiment of the incarnation.

- *Don't be afraid of silence.* Embrace silence, however awkward it may feel. Kate Bower's wise words are important here: "The truth is that no one knows what to say. It's awkward. Pain is awkward. Tragedy is awkward. People's weird, suffering bodies are awkward. But take the advice of one man who wrote to me with his policy: Show up and shut up."[30]

I don't understand the why of suffering. I am still learning to ask, *Where is God?* rather than, *Why did God allow this to happen?* It may be Good Friday in our lives today, but I'm confident that Easter Sunday is coming—maybe not tomorrow or next week or next month, but it's coming. The purpose of the cross and resurrection is not to explain the existence of suffering or evil but to assure us that God is with us in the midst of our deepest pain and has overcome death by raising Jesus from the dead: "Christian hope is confidence that the same God who suffered in his Son and raised him from the grave will finish what he has begun."[31] May each of us be the embodiment of such hope to one another. Amen.

---

30. Bowler, *Everything Happens for a Reason and Other Lies I've Loved,* 175.

31. Al Truesdale, *If God Is God Then Why? Letters from New York City* (Kansas City, MO: Beacon Hill Press of Kansas City, 2002), 85.

FOR REFLECTION

- When have you experienced the church as a means of grace when you or a loved one has suffered?
- How can you and your church be a means of grace to those who suffer in your local community?
- What means of grace have sustained you or a loved one when you have experienced devastating loss?
- Our theology (understanding of God) informs our responses to those who suffer. As we represent Christ to the suffering, what are we to say or not to say? How do we know which actions are helpful or hurtful? Discuss with a small group or Sunday school class appropriate and inappropriate responses to those who suffer.
- Dietrich Bonhoeffer said, "Only the suffering God can help."[32] How does it sustain your faith to know that God suffers with you and with others who suffer?
- Biblical lament provides a language with which to express our grief and inability to explain rationally why suffering occurs. How has lament been a means of grace to you during times of deep pain?

---

32. Dietrich Bonhoeffer, *Letters and Papers from Prison*, in *Works*, Vol. 8 (Philadelphia: Fortress Press, 2010), 479.

SEEING GOD IN ALL THINGS

Fuel for a More Resilient Life

RESILIENCE TIP

Resilient people learn to see God in all things in such a way that their lives are lived from a vital spring of gratitude, beauty, joy, and delight.

To behold God in all things is to live in complete joy.
> —*Julian of Norwich,* The Showings of Julian of Norwich

Thankfulness is the quickest path to joy.
> —*Jefferson Bethke,* Jesus > Religion

Let me keep company always with those who say "Look!" and laugh in astonishment and bow their heads.
> —*Mary Oliver,* "Mysteries, Yes"

Christ plays in ten thousand places, lovely in limbs, and lovely in eyes not his.
> —*Gerard Manley Hopkins,* "As Kingfishers Catch Fire"

We seldom notice how each day is a holy place where the eucharist of the ordinary happens, transforming our broken fragments into an eternal continuity that keeps us.
> —*John O'Donohue,* To Bless the Space between Us

If I were called upon to state in a few words the essence of everything I was trying to say as a novelist and as a preacher, it would be something like this: Listen to your life. See it for the fathomless mystery that it is. In the boredom and pain of it no less than in the excitement and gladness: touch, taste, smell your way to the holy and hidden heart of it because in the last analysis all moments are key moments, and life itself is grace.

—*Frederick Buechner,* Listening to Your Life

Most of us are beginners when it comes to paying attention to God's presence in the ordinary moments of life. We may discern obvious things but miss the small graces in daily life—especially those that appear during trying times. It takes regular practice to become the kind of people who are attentive to God's presence in each moment. This kind of seeing requires that we develop what I'm calling a sacramental imagination.[1] We develop sacramental imagination through the practice of "finding God in all things."[2] A sacramental imagination is the ability to see the presence of God precisely in those moments of life that seem too ordinary or painful to yield anything of lasting value.[3] Resilient people cultivate a sacramental vision of everyday life by recognizing and responding to God's moment-by-moment presence with gratitude, joy, and delight.

We see a sacramental imagination at work in the following:

---

1. The word "sacramental" comes from the Latin word *sacer*, meaning "holy." We use the word "sacred" to refer to anything that is set apart for God's service. The Bible is a "sacred text," for example. Sometimes music used in church worship is called "sacred music."

2. This phrase comes from Saint Ignatius of Loyola, the founder of the Jesuits. Similar to John Wesley's doctrine of prevenient grace, Ignatius maintained that God is active and present in every person and in all creation. See https://www.jesuits.global/spirituality/finding-god-in-all-things.

3. A classic book on this topic was written in the 1700s by Jean-Pierre De Caussade. See *The Sacrament of the Present Moment*, trans. Kitty Muggeridge (San Francisco: HarperSanFrancisco, 1982).

"Look at the birds of the air: they neither sow nor reap nor gather into barns, and yet your heavenly Father feeds them. Are you not of more value than they?"

—*Matthew 6:26, NRSVUE*

"And why do you worry about clothing? Consider the lilies of the field, how they grow; they neither toil nor spin."

—*Matthew 6:28, NRSVUE*

"God is always present to us and to all things; it is that we, like a blind person, do not have the eyes to see."

—*Saint Augustine*

"The pure in heart see all things full of God."

—*John Wesley*[4]

"We are living in a world that is absolutely transparent, and God is shining through all the time."

—*Thomas Merton*[5]

"If we live sacramentally, where we are intentionally paying attention to the activity and grace of God in everyday life, we will see it."

—*Dean Nelson*[6]

After God created the heavens and the earth and Adam and Eve, "God saw all that he had made, and it was very good" (Genesis 1:31a). Even with the woundedness we experience so often in our world, God's creation remains "very good." Robert Benson observes, "There is no ground that is not holy ground. All the places of our lives are sanctuaries; some of them just happen

---

4. Wesley, "Sermon on the Mount, III," *The Works of John Wesley, Sermons I, 1–33* (Nashville: Abingdon, 1984), 513. A little later in the same sermon Wesley says, "God is in all things, and . . . we are to see the Creator in the glass of every creature. . . . We should use and look upon nothing as separate from God, which is indeed a kind of practical atheism" (516–17).

5. Merton, *Thomas Merton: Essential Writings* (Maryknoll, NY: Orbis Books, 2000), 70.

6. Dean Nelson, *God Hides in Plain Sight: How to See the Sacred in a Chaotic World* (Grand Rapids: Brazos Press, 2009), 26.

to have steeples."[7] God is not contained within the four walls of a church. Recognizing God in all of life has the potential to transform our day-to-day lives. As we see God more clearly in our lives, we will experience a richer sense of purpose. We will find fresh energy for living. We will become more resilient. We will find joy bubbling up within us. We will see God's captivating and transforming beauty all around us.

Life, in all its many-splendored dimensions, manifests God's gracious presence. Creation itself is transparent to God. This is what is sometimes called the sacramental nature of life. Life is like a sacrament where every person, event, thing, and aspect of nature is illuminated by God's loving presence. Do we have the eyes to see it? Elizabeth Barrett Browning's poem "Aurora Leigh" helps us see God's presence in the common, easily overlooked, ordinary moments of our days:

> Earth's crammed with heaven,
> And every common bush afire with God;
> But only he who sees, takes off his shoes,
> The rest sit round it and pluck blackberries,
> And daub their natural faces unaware . . .[8]

Browning expands our theological vision to recognize that every moment of our lives is "crammed" with God, if we have the eyes to see it. A bush we walk by several times a day without noticing is truly "afire with God." Browning's poem alludes to Moses's vision of God in the burning bush (see Exodus 3:1–5). How many times did Moses walk by the same bush before he noticed it was "afire with God"? And where would we be if Moses had never stopped to take a closer look? Each day is our opportunity to do

---

7. Robert Benson, *Between the Dreaming and the Coming True: The Road Home to God* (New York: Putnum Inc., 1996), 141.

8. Elizabeth Barrett Browning, "Aurora Leigh," *The Oxford Book of English Mystical Verse*, ed. Nicholson and Lee (1917), http://www.bartleby.com/236/86.html.

just as Moses did: to behold the all-too-ordinary bushes of our lives that are "afire with God."

Macrina Wiederkehr, a Benedictine nun, says that the daily experiences of God in the ordinary moments of life are like crumbs. We don't often get to see the whole loaf; but, as the Syrophoenician women told Jesus (see Mark 7:24–30), even crumbs are nourishing. Wiederkehr calls these "stepping stones to holiness":

> There is nothing—no thing, no person, no experience, no thought, no joy or pain—that cannot be harvested and used for nourishment on our journey to God. What I am suggesting here is that everything in your life is a stepping stone to holiness if only you recognize that you do have within you the grace to be present to each moment. . . . Each experience, every thought, every word, every person in your life is a part of a larger picture of your growth. That's why I call them crumbs. They are not the whole loaf, but they can be nourishing if you give them your real presence. Let everything energize you. Let everything bless you. Even your limping can bless you. All too often we bemoan our imperfections rather than embrace them as part of the process by which we are brought to God.[9]

A sacramental understanding of life sees that every person, event, and creature is illuminated by God's presence. There is no place that God is not. God's presence is all around us. This is what theologians refer to as the omnipresence of God—or God's *everywhereness*. Thomas Merton puts it this way:

> We are living in a world that is absolutely transparent, and God is shining through it all the time. This is not just a fable or a nice story. . . . God manifests himself everywhere, in everything—in people and in things and in nature and in events and so forth. So that it becomes very obvious that he is everywhere, he is in

9. Macrina Wiederkehr, *A Tree Full of Angels: Seeing the Holy in the Ordinary* (San Francisco: HarperSanFrancisco, 1995), 26–27.

SEEING GOD IN ALL THINGS

everything, and we cannot be without him. You cannot be without God. It's impossible, it's just simply impossible.[10]

God told Moses at the burning bush, "Take off your sandals, for the place where you are standing is holy ground" (Exodus 3:5). Isaiah experienced this when, during his vision of God in the temple, he saw seraphim exclaim, "Holy, holy, holy is the LORD Almighty; the whole earth is full of his glory" (Isaiah 6:3). The psalmist expressed something similar when praising God: "The earth is filled with your love, LORD" (119:64). Wherever we are, God's love circulates through every part of creation. A sacramental imagination of life fills us with daily joy. The sense of God's everywhereness can sustain us during the most trying times of life.

Sandwiches as Sacraments

In 1996 Andre Dubus stopped to help two motorists with disabilities on the side of a Massachusetts highway, then was struck by a passing car, costing him one leg and the use of the other. Dubus was a Catholic writer from the south who had made a career writing stories in which his characters experience various accidents that give them desperately needed wake-up calls. After his own debilitating accident, Dubus continued to write and reflect on God's presence in his daily life, referring to the sacraments of daily life as an outward sign of God's love.[11] He expanded his Roman Catholic tradition's vision of seven sacraments in the affirmation that sacraments can be found everywhere: "There are seven times seventy sacraments, to infinity." He saw God's holy love in the simple act of making sandwiches for his daughters after

---

10. Merton, *Essential Writings*, 70.

11. The traditional definition of a sacrament is "an outward sign of inward grace." Protestants affirm two sacraments, baptism and Communion. Roman Catholics recognize seven sacraments: baptism, confirmation, Eucharist, reconciliation, anointing of the sick, marriage, and holy orders.

his accident led him to focus on every action he took.[12] Dubus described what this looked like in his daily routine:

> On Tuesdays when I make lunches for my girls, I focus on this: the sandwiches are sacraments. Not the miracle of transubstantiation, but certainly parallel with it, moving in the same direction. If I could give my children my body to eat, again and again without losing it, my body like the loaves and fishes going endlessly into mouths and stomachs, I would do it. And each motion is a sacrament, this holding of plastic bags, of knives, of bread, of cutting board, this pushing of the chair, this spreading of mustard on bread, this trimming of liverwurst, of ham. All sacraments, as putting the lunches into a zippered book bag is, and going down my six ramps to my car is.[13]

In spite of his devastating accident—or possibly because of it— Dubus viewed the ordinary and sometimes excruciatingly painful moments of his life in light of the presence of God. Dubus's life was messy. He was married and divorced three times and lived with chronic pain. Despite multiple challenges, he developed the habit of recognizing every action of his life as a sacrament, a reminder of the real presence of God that would never leave or forsake him.

I first read about Dubus's story when our children were school age. His sacramental vision of life helped open my eyes to my everyday reality: *My house is full of the glory of God!* My kids were full of mischief, but they were also full of the glory of God. How easy it is to miss this, especially in the midst of our ordinary, day-in-day-out lives at home. It's all too easy to grumble inwardly, if not outwardly, about fixing lunches, cooking dinner, doing the dishes, cleaning up messes, doing homework, putting kids to bed, mowing the lawn, or fixing things that break.

---

12. Christina Bieber, "Living Like a Man: Andre Dubus and the Lessons of Brokenness," *Books & Culture: A Christian Review* (May/June 2003), http://www.booksand-culture.com/articles/2003/mayjun/6.8.html.

13. Andre Dubus, *Meditations from a Movable Chair* (New York: Alfred Knopf, 1998), 89.

Our daily lives can indeed be stepping stones to holiness. These are sacramental acts, gracious invitations from God to love and serve those we love most in this world. How would it make a difference in the way we live our lives if we daily reminded ourselves: *My world is full of the glory of God. My life is illumined by God's holiness.* We are all works in progress here. I admit that too often I still miss the stepping stones to holiness that are right under my nose.

None of us is guaranteed another day. We are only given today, and this moment in particular. As the old saying goes, yesterday is history. Tomorrow is a mystery. Today is a gift. That's why it's called "the present." G. K. Chesterton's wise words often come to mind as I try to be grateful for the gifts of this day and mindful that others haven't had an opportunity for another day:

> *Here dies another day*
> *During which I have had eyes, ears, hands*
> *And the great world round me;*
> *And with tomorrow begins another.*
> *Why am I allowed two?*[14]

Some time ago, after Shelly and I took Annie to a doctor's appointment, we ate lunch in the Denver Children's Hospital cafeteria. As we were waiting for our food, Shelly noticed the extra care the young man waiting on us was taking to make sure everything was in just the right place on her plate—the salad greens here, the noodles there, the sauce just so. She told him, "I really like the way you put the plate together. Your presentation is beautiful." The young man seemed uncommonly grateful that Shelly took a minute to notice his special effort and the pride he took in his work. Truly, the earth is filled with the glory of God.

---

14. G. K. Chesterton, "Evening," *The Collected Works of G. K. Chesterton* (San Francisco: Ignatius Press, 1986), 38.

Unwrapped Pennies All around Us

In *Pilgrim at Tinker Creek*, Annie Dillard shares about a game she used to play. When she was six or seven, she liked to hide her precious pennies in nooks and crannies in trees or cracks in sidewalks. Knowing these clever places were too subtle for the average person to find, she drew huge chalk arrows pointing toward the hidden pennies. After she learned to write, she "labeled the arrows: SURPRISE AHEAD or MONEY THIS WAY."[15] The young Dillard was filled with anticipation as she imagined a passerby coming upon one of her gratuitous arrows leading to a treasured penny, a gift from an unseen hand. As an adult she reflects on the relevance of hiding pennies as a child for the way we see the world:

> It is still the first week in January and I've got great plans. I've been thinking about seeing. There are lots of things to see, unwrapped gifts and free surprises. The world is fairly studded and strewn with pennies cast broadside from a generous hand. But—and this is the point—who gets excited by a mere penny? If you follow one arrow, if you crouch motionless on a bank to watch a tremulous ripple thrill on the water and are rewarded with the sight of a muskrat kit paddling from its den, will you count that sight a chip of copper only, and go your rueful way? It is dire poverty indeed when a [person] is so malnourished and fatigued [they] won't stoop to pick up a penny. But if you cultivate a healthy poverty and simplicity, so that finding a penny will literally make your day, then, since the world is in fact planted in pennies, you have with your poverty bought a lifetime of days. It is that simple. *What you see is what you get.*[16]

What do we see? Is our world one of scarcity where there is only so much to go around? Or is it one of abundance, where a

---

15. Annie Dillard, *Pilgrim at Tinker Creek* (New York: HarperPerennial, 1974), 15.
16. Dillard, *Pilgrim at Tinker Creek*, 15.

few dried fish and loaves of bread are enough to feed thousands and there are pennies all around just waiting to be discovered?

Gratitude

One of the most effective practices for growing deeper roots of resilience is gratitude. The habit of gratitude helps us manage depression, disappointment, anxiety, and resentment.[17] It's no wonder that Scripture exhorts us to "give thanks" to God 48 times. The words "thank," "thankfulness," and "thanksgiving" occur in various contexts in Scripture 133 times.

German Christian mystic Meister Eckhart (c. 1260–1328) is thought to have said of the importance of gratitude in a life of prayer: "If the only prayer you said was thank you, that would be enough." No matter what I'm feeling at the beginning of Shelly's and my daily two-mile walks with our dogs along the river, I eventually sense the words "thank you, thank you, thank you" spontaneously rising up within me. The apostle Paul recognized that gratitude and prayer go hand in glove: "Pray continually, give thanks in all circumstances; for this is God's will for you in Christ Jesus" (1 Thessalonians 5:17–18).

The gratitude that any of us experience in life is almost always gratitude in spite of less than favorable circumstances. If we wait to practice gratitude until everything is going perfectly, we will never become people of gratitude. The habit of gratitude enables us to be thankful in the midst of the life we have been given—not the life we imagined as idealistic eighteen-year-olds but the one that time, chance, choice, and circumstances have given us. Gratitude, like resilience, is learned. It is a means of grace that we must practice every day. Those of us who are parents know that children are not born with gratitude but must be coached.

---

17. For a terrific book on how practicing gratitude can make us happier, see Robert A. Emmons, *Thanks! How Practicing Gratitude Can Make You Happier* (Boston: Houghton Mifflin Company, 2007).

I should note that gratitude does not always come naturally to parents either.

When I consider those who have mentored me in gratitude, the first who comes to mind is my childhood dog, Duke.[18] My first memory of Duke is from the gray Pacific Northwest winter day my stepfather and I went to adopt him when I was eight. As we drove up to a run-down old farmhouse with more mud than grass in the yard, I noticed a skin-and-bones dog with an ugly red growth in the corner of his left eye, tied up to the side of the house in pouring rain with no place for shelter. My heart sank as I thought, *This can't be the dog we've come to see!* Drenched by incessant rain and splattered with mud, he hardly resembled the handsome, white-and-butterscotch, six-year-old English pointer he was. Later we found out he was a registered English pointer with the name "Mark of Abelia." Such a regal name did not fit such a bedraggled dog. It hardly seemed possible.

We threw down some blankets in the backseat of our car, and the dog who became Duke gladly hopped in, his tail wagging sixty miles an hour and flinging mud all over me and the car. At home we gave Duke a bath. He grunted in ecstasy as we dried him off. He soaked up every ounce of affection. It was as if no one had paid attention to him for years. Once he was cleaned up, he didn't look nearly so bedraggled. Duke became part of our family that afternoon, and he and I soon became the best of friends.

Duke's favorite thing in life, other than eating and playing with his red rubber squeaker rat (the one we buried with him when he died of intestinal cancer four years later), was getting new straw for his bed. His bed was a four-by-four plywood box we placed in a corner of the garage. I'm not sure why we used straw instead of blankets, but that's what we used—and he loved it. In order to make his bed fluffy, we peeled small flakes of straw from a bale, pulling

---

18. For a wonderful book on the gift of dogs, see Andrew Root, *The Grace of Dogs: A Boy, a Black Lab, and a Father's Search for the Canine Soul* (Colorado Springs: Convergent Books, 2017).

them apart to make a cozy nest. Duke, of course, had to be in the midst of the making of his bed, grunting and groaning with sheer delight—and sneezing from the dust. When all the straw had been put in his bed and most of the dust had settled, he turned around and around until the straw was just like he wanted it. As he lay securely in his nest, his tail thumping appreciatively, his bright eyes signaled his gratitude. If dogs can smile, he grinned from ear to ear.

Not all dogs are like Duke. At the same time we had Duke, we had another English pointer, Susie, who lived a pampered life. Susie had her good points, but she was often temperamental, demanding, and grew increasingly crotchety the older she became. I've known some people like Susie. Maybe you have too.

I'm not a dog psychologist, but I believe Duke's infectious gratitude came from his remembrance of the times when he had nothing—no shelter, no love, little food. He never forgot where he came from. Gratitude flowed from him for any sign of love or kindness shown to him. Even in the last days of his life, when cancer made him sick and unable to keep food down, I'd pet him and his tail would still go thump, thump, thump. Duke lived and died grateful. I'm trying to do the same. Even though life is sometimes difficult, I still have so much to be grateful for—don't we all?

As my wife has continued to heal from the brain surgery I mentioned in the preface, there have been good days and bad days and, slowly, better days. There has been the loss of her ear-to-ear smile that I have always treasured—and still see smiling back at me in old pictures. I miss her full-faced smile—and she does too—but she is alive and has all her mental faculties. She is, in all the ways I love most, the Shelly she has always been—funny, grateful, intelligent, compassionate, and fiercely resilient. Shelly has shared her post-surgery progress every month or so on Facebook. She has chosen not to give the "glittering image"[19] story of her recovery but has shared pictures of the droopy side

19. I first became familiar with this phrase from reading Susan Howatch's engaging novel *Glittering Images* (New York: Ballantine Books, 1995). I highly recommend this

of her face. The droopiness, much like Bell's palsy, was caused by a cranial nerve that was stunned during surgery. Many family and friends have thanked Shelly for her vulnerability in sharing her unvarnished, incomplete recovery.

In the meantime, we do our best to lean into joy and practice gratitude for what we still have rather than obsess about what may never return. We count our blessings so we do not fixate on our losses. As we add and multiply the gratitude we feel for so many things in our lives, new ways of thinking and feeling begin to appear. We are learning to tell ourselves a story that counters the way we feel some days. In chapter 6, I talked about the apostle Paul's pregnant phrase "in Christ" that can be so helpful as we seek to manage depression. This is where Shelly and I seek to rest—in the hard-won hope that, because Christ is in us and all around us, our problems are not permanent or pervasive. We are learning to see our lives with fresh eyes.

Scripture does not teach that our lives will be a happily-ever-after fairy tale where we never grow old, develop wrinkles, get sick, or die. But the story of God is indeed one of hopeful resilience in the face of illness, suffering, and disappointment. Like the Israelites stuck in Babylonian captivity, where there seemed to be no way out of exile, God always makes a way for God's people (Isaiah 43:16–19). It may be a different way than we imagined or prayed for, but God always makes a way, even through tear-stained eyes and broken hearts. When we need it the most and expect it the least, the resurrected Christ appears to us on the dusty, despair-filled roads of our lives and speaks peace and hope to us (Luke 24:13–35). These are the kinds of stories that anchor us as Christ followers when the storms of life threaten to sink us.

The habit of gratitude strengthens the grip of Christlike resilience in the face of circumstances that might otherwise overwhelm us. Gratitude provides insulation from the bumps and bruises of

---

book and the others in the series. I've learned more about the integration of spirituality and psychology from Howatch than from any other author.

life. It's not that gratitude takes away heartache or the negativity that nags at all of us. Gratitude enables us to reframe our circumstances. Gratitude helps us tell a broader story where our losses or pain are no longer the central characters. Yes, there's still pain, but pain is not the only thing or even the main thing about our lives. In the midst of the rubble of our lives, these three always remain: faith, hope, and love (1 Corinthians 13:13). It's true that we never give thanks *for* painful and heartbreaking things that happen to us. But if we learn to find ways to give thanks *in the midst of* such circumstances, slowly the pain we feel today will eventually grow into loving gratitude tomorrow.

Over the years I've slowly learned to be grateful for what I've learned about God, myself, and others through experiences I never imagined had anything to teach me. The death of my father still has an edge of deep sadness to it almost forty years later. But because of it, I've grown to be a more compassionate presence with those who suffer. I've developed the ability to walk with others through their own "valley of the shadow of death" (Psalm 23:4, KJV). The words of the apostle Paul resonate in my soul: "Praise be to the God and Father of our Lord Jesus Christ, the Father of compassion and the God of all comfort, who comforts us in all our troubles, so that we can comfort those in any trouble with the comfort we ourselves receive from God" (2 Corinthians 1:3–4).

Like the rings of a tree, the loss I still feel over my father's death has become part of me. It will remain a significant ring of my life until my own death. Then there was depression. It took many years for me to develop any kind of gratitude for this dark night of the soul. Like so many others who've gone through depression and come out the other side, God turned my ashes into beauty and mourning into joy (Isaiah 61:3). What was once the most shameful experience of my life has become one of the most important experiences I have for sharing hope with those who struggle with burnout and depression.

When Annie was going through the darkest times of her bone disease, it was impossible to be grateful. Her suffering knocked the wind out of us. It took a long time to get our breath back. There's no way to speed healing or grief. They take as long as they take. One thing Annie's pain eventually showed us was to give thanks for daily blessings, however small they were. It helped us live in the moment rather than obsess about what tomorrow might bring. It taught us the importance of giving thanks for this day, this breath, this hug, this laugh, this meal together—because there might not be another one. It helped me see me that, however horrible life may sometimes be, I need to lean daily into the hope of the gospel. Slowly I'm learning that gratitude is the only way to live—and the only way to survive, and enter into the "life that is truly life" (1 Timothy 6:19).

We can't change our circumstances. We will need to learn how to give thanks for imperfect gifts—because there is no such thing as a perfect, problem-free, pain-free life. We can't control what other people do or don't do. But by the grace of God we can, moment by moment, begin to choose an attitude of gratitude. This is what resilient people have learned to do. We won't always get it right, but with regular practice the arc of our lives will begin to bend in the direction of gratitude.

Beauty

One of the chief ways that God's holiness expresses itself, other than love, is through beauty. God's holiness is a never-ceasing, over-flowing stream of love and beauty. Just as we affirm that God is love, so we can also say God is beauty. In several places in the psalms, God's holiness and beauty are presented side by side, as if they are two sides of the same coin (see 29:2; 65; 96:9; and 110:3, for example). God-created beauty, wherever we encounter it, is intricately interconnected with the everywhere-present, always-bubbling-up presence of God—or what Wesleyans refer to as prevenient grace.

The beauty we observe throughout creation is the tangible, physical, audible, fragrant, and delicious expression of God's love for all creation.[20] It may help to think of beauty as the physical reflection of God's loving presence circulating through all created things. This is where a sacramental imagination is so important for sustaining us in good times and bad. Julian of Norwich (c. 1342–1416) recognized this very thing when she wrote, "To behold God in all things is to live in complete joy."[21] How does beholding God in all things lead us to complete joy? Seeing God in all things, people, and places is a constant reminder that we are never alone. Wherever we go, whatever circumstances in which we find ourselves, God is constantly with us, loving us, strengthening us, healing us.

Our feelings may tell us another story, however. As we look at our circumstances, it may appear that nothing is changing. But because God's character is holy love, God has promised never to leave or forsake us (Deuteronomy 31:6; Hebrews 13:5). And because God is holy love, we are assured that all creation is filled with God's loving presence (Isaiah 6:3b; Psalm 119:64). The doctrine of prevenient grace affirms that God is with us, even to the very depths of our DNA. Our belief that Christ—the suffering, resurrecting one—is always with us, our loved ones, and those who experience failure, abuse, illness, and oppression of any kind enables us to tell stories of hope, redemption, and resurrection. Stories of hope sustain us and make us more resilient in the face of the storms of life.

We may have never thought of it this way before, but God communicates God's love to us through our five senses of taste, touch, smell, sight, and hearing. Our senses offer important clues for recognizing the beauty of God. Think of sunrises and sunsets,

---

20. See Wirzba, *Food and Faith: A Theology of Eating* (Cambridge: Cambridge University Press, 2019). See also Wirzba, *This Sacred Life: Humanity's Place in a Wounded World* (London: Oxford University Press, 2021).

21. Mirabai Starr, *The Showings of Julian of Norwich: A New Translation* (Charlottesville, VA: Hampton Roads, 2013), 84.

walks along a beach. The smile and embrace of a loved one. The sound of wind rustling through aspen leaves. The sweet fragrance or taste of sun-ripened fruit, the feel of its juice running down our chin. The sound of pounding ocean surf. The crunch of dried leaves underfoot in the fall. The voice, laugh, or touch of a loved one. The beauty of a delicious meal shared with loved ones. All these experiences are reminders of God's constant presence and care for us and all creation.

Beauty as a means of grace is essential to living fully alive, resilient lives. Notice that the psalmist says in Psalm 34, "Taste and see that the LORD is good" (v. 8). The psalmist knew that delicious food comforts us and reminds us of God's caretaking of our lives. Good food reminds us that God's beauty sustains us on a daily basis. A delectable meal shared with loved ones, filled with laughter and full of joy, becomes a means of grace for the long journey ahead.

There are many wounded places and people in the world, but God's beauty gives us hope and energy to join hands with God in praying and working for the healing and beautification of all things in Christ.[22] Every time we behold beauty, we are reminded that God is the creator and sustainer of all things. Since God sustains earth, the universe, and everything we humans know and don't know, we can be confident that God also sustains *us*. Jesus reminds us of God's care in Matthew 6 when he points to the birds of the air and the flowers of the field as illustrations of God's love made physical, visible, fragrant, and audible. Jesus's message is, if God takes care of birds and flowers, then how much more will he take care of us? "Therefore," Jesus says, "do not worry about tomorrow, for tomorrow will worry about itself. Each day has enough trouble of its own" (v. 34). Beauty is an effective antidote to worry—and so many other things.

Beauty sustains us in the midst of tough times. Many years ago, when I was a burned-out and depressed pastor, riding my

---

22. Wirzba, *This Sacred Life*, 225.

mountain bike through all four seasons in Colorado helped heal my depression. It wasn't the only thing that helped, but it was a very important tributary of healing. The wind, the sun, the rain, the sleet, and the snow—as one season moved into another—tethered me to God in a way that nothing else did at the time. During this time I experienced God in creation via my five senses. I felt the fingers of the freezing rain rake my cheeks. My body ached as I pedaled up steep hills. I smelled the sweet, wet grass of spring. I heard the frogs croak. I tasted the bugs that flew into my mouth when I forgot to close it. I saw the leaves bud, leaf, and turn breathtaking shades of red, yellow, and orange, before dropping to the ground. The change in seasons gave me hope that my season of depression might eventually change. The wilderness explorer John Muir is reported to have said along these lines, "And into the forest I go, to lose my mind and find my soul."[23] In the beauty of God's creation is where I find my soul as well.

Beauty heals. We don't have to go for a bike ride or march off into the forest to find the beauty we need. Such beauty is often within reach in our own homes. My maternal grandmother suffered from depression during the dark, dreary winter days of the Pacific Northwest. One thing that kept her going was her crop of beloved African violets, which she tended as if they were her children. Shelly and I love African violets as well. We have a mother plant that we received more than thirty years ago from the grandmother of a friend. It continues to thrive and radiate beauty all year long.

Beauty, especially in dark times, gives us hope that a brighter day will dawn. Barbara Kingsolver writes about how common beauty has filled her with the joy to learn how to be in love with her life again:

> In my own worst seasons I've come back from the colorless world of despair by forcing myself to look hard, for a long time, at a

---

23. John Muir is credited with making significant contributions to the creation of the National Park system in the United States and the founding of the Sierra Club.

single glorious thing: a flame of red geranium outside my bed-room window. And then another: my daughter in a yellow dress. And another: the perfect outline of a full, dark sphere behind the crescent moon. Until I learned to be in love with my life again. Like a stroke victim retraining new parts of the brain to grasp lost skills, I have taught myself joy, over and over again.[24]

Kingsolver explains so well how experiencing the beauty of God's creation and having it wash over me again and again retrains my brain to find hope again.

I invite you to stop, look, listen, sip, sniff, taste, touch, hear, and observe beauty in the everyday moments of your life. As you do so, I'm confident you will find worry turning into trust, despair giving way to hope, and sorrow gradually becoming joy. These movements are not instantaneous. Like most worthwhile things—and here we're talking about character, becoming the kind of people who habitually seek out God's presence in daily life, especially in beautiful things—it will take intentional practice, patience, and perseverance.

The first time I began to reflect on how God is truly present in all creation and creatures was as a seminary student at Nazarene Theological Seminary. One of my professors pointed out one day in class that the hymn "Joyful, Joyful, We Adore Thee" is a song about prevenient grace—God's saving presence reflected in all creatures and creation. His comment didn't have much to do with the class he was teaching, but it was as if a light bulb went on in my mind. I had never considered how God shines through all created things or how they are lit up by God's presence. I've been seeking to unpack the implications of that insight ever since. Take a look at the words of that hymn:

> *Joyful, joyful, we adore thee, God of glory, Lord of love;*
> *Hearts unfold like flowers before thee, opening to the sun*
> *above.*

---

24. Barbara Kingsolver, *High Tide: Essays from Now or Never* (New York: Harper-Collins, 1995), 15.

Melt the clouds of sin and sadness; drive the dark of doubt
away.
Giver of immortal gladness, fill us with the light of day!

All thy works with joy surround thee; earth and heaven re-
flect thy rays;
Stars and angels sing around thee, center of unbroken praise.
Field and forest, vale and mountain, flowery meadow, flash-
ing sea,
Chanting bird and flowing fountain call us to rejoice in thee.[25]

Earth and heaven reflect the rays of God's gracious presence. Once we see this, we can never not see it.

Regularly paying attention to the fingerprints of God in creation builds resilience. We may not be able to get outside every day due to weather or other circumstances, but any time we can be in God's good creation is a means of grace. In nature we give thanks. We pray. We are filled with gratitude. Nature heals us. Wendell Berry describes how he is drawn to nature when he despairs or worries:

When despair for the world grows in me and I wake in the night at the least sound in fear of what my life and my children's lives may be, I go and lie down where the wood drake rests in his beauty on the water, and the great heron feeds. I come into the peace of wild things who do not tax their lives with forethought of grief. I come into the presence of still water. And I feel above me the day-blind stars waiting with their light. For a time I rest in the grace of the world, and am free.[26]

God constantly speaks to us through creation: "The heavens declare the glory of God; the skies proclaim the work of his hands.

---

25. Ludwig van Beethoven (music, 1824) and Henry van Dyke (words, 1907), "Joyful, Joyful, We Adore Thee," *Sing to the Lord: Hymnal* (Kansas City, MO: Lillenas Publishing Co., 1993), #17.

26. Berry, "The Peace of Wild Things," *The Selected Poems of Wendell Berry*, 30.

Day after day they pour forth speech; night after night they reveal knowledge" (Psalm 19:1–2). Do we have the ears to hear the voice of God in creation? Mary Oliver puts it this way: "When I am among the trees . . . they give off such hints of gladness. I would almost say that they save me, and daily."[27] Oliver, a Christian, is not saying that trees save us in place of Christ's saving work. She's saying that they save us with a small "s." What is saving you these days? Yes, Jesus is the one who Saves us, but God also uses trees, flowers, dogs, cats, and even donkeys to save us (as the prophet Balaam discovered in Numbers 22:21–39).

A robust incarnational theology helps us see that God uses myriad ways to save us, to keep going when we'd rather give up, including God's own creation. In this sense, the life of Christian holiness is a call to beauty—to experience beauty, yes, but also to reflect it, to illuminate the world by living lives of winsome moral beauty—to live our lives in such lavish generosity, kindness, and compassion that we are living witnesses to the beautiful news of Christ. Beauty attracts, whether it's a flower, a waterfall, a demonstration of love toward the marginalized, or a life lived well.

Incarnational Imagination

All of creation and those of us who inhabit it bear God's image. Who of us standing on a beach overlooking the setting sun has not exclaimed something like, "What a wonderful world you've created, God! Thank you! Thank you! Thank you!" One of the reasons the song made popular by Louis Armstrong, "What a Wonderful World," has *been* so popular over the years is that it calls our attention to the beauty in the world. It's hard not to get caught up in the ugliness, strife, and injustices we hear far too much of. We need songs like this that remind us that sin and injustice do not have the final word.

---

27. Mary Oliver, "When I Am among the Trees," *Devotions: The Selected Poems of Mary Oliver* (New York: Penguin Press, 2017), 123.

Even so, it's tempting to ask, *How can we spare the time to go into nature and notice beauty when there is so much needless suffering and injustice in the world?* To respond to a question like this, I find myself often turning to poets: the psalmist, Mary Oliver, Wendell Berry, Jack Gilbert, and others. Mary Oliver asks the question many of us may ask when pain is weighing heavily upon us: "If the world were only pain and logic, who would want it?"[28] Poet Jack Gilbert responds to such a concern in "A Brief for the Defense":

> If we deny our happiness, resist our satisfaction,
> we lessen the importance of their deprivation.
> We must risk delight. We can do without pleasure,
> but not delight. Not enjoyment. We must have
> the stubbornness to accept our gladness in the ruthless
> furnace of this world. To make injustice the only
> measure of our attention is to praise the Devil.[29]

You may need to read the lines I've included from Gilbert's poem a few times. The phrase my mind keeps circling back around to is the last one: "To make injustice the only measure of our attention is to praise the Devil." Just as we cannot live one moment without hope, life is not worth living without delight and joy.

To live fully alive lives as God's creative and redemptive agents in the world means that yes, we acknowledge, weep, and work to overcome injustice. But we are also fully aware that, without beauty and the joy it produces, we will not have the strength of heart to join hands with God for the healing of our sin-wounded world. Anne Lamott speaks of the importance of joy, particularly in troubling times: "Joy is portable. Joy is a habit, and . . . it can be a radical act."[30] When we are filled with joy, we take it with us wherever we go. The more we lean into joy, the easier the habit

---

28. Oliver, "Singapore," *Devotions*, 327.

29. Jack Gilbert, "A Brief for the Defense," *Joy: 100 Poems*, ed. Christian Wiman (New Haven, CT: Yale University Press, 2018), 36.

30. Lamott, *Almost Everything: Notes on Hope* (New York: Riverhead Books, 2018), 56.

of joy is to develop. As our life bumps into the lives of others, some of our joy will spill onto them.

Joy is the oxygen that breathes life into our lungs in the midst of the complexities, conundrums, and contradictions of life that threaten to overwhelm us. Joy makes it possible for us to keep going no matter the circumstances of our lives.[31] As Wendell Berry urges us, "Laughter is immeasurable. Be joyful though you have considered all the facts."[32] Berry is saying that joy is irreplaceable fuel for resilience. Joy is the sheer delight of fulfilling the purpose for which we were made. Joy is serendipity—the unexpected pleasure of the radiance of a flower, the embrace of a loved one, listening to a favorite song, or eating something delicious.

Without joy we grow world-weary and can be tempted to give up far more easily than when our joy tank is overflowing. The joy that comes from Christ can even overcome evil: "[Joy] is a felt sense in our bodies. In the face of horrors visited upon our world daily, in the struggle to protect our loved ones, choosing to let in joy is a revolutionary act. Joy returns us to everything good and beautiful and worth fighting for. It gives us energy for the long labor. . . . Joy is the gift of love: it makes the labor an end in itself. I believe laboring in joy is the meaning of life.[33] With joy, the overwhelming becomes endurable; resilience becomes sustainable. Joy is the delight that my life and your life matter—and the lives of all God's beloved children. Joy gives us the stamina to continue to work for God's kingdom when results are small or few and far between. Joy fills our lungs with the oxygen necessary to keep going when we feel we can't go any further. Jesus breathes his life into us "so that my joy may be in you and that your joy may be complete" (John 15:11)—even

---

31. For a timely book on joy in uncertain times, see Jeren Rowell, *Joy: Choosing Hope in an Age of Uncertainty* (Kansas City, MO: The Foundry Publishing, 2022).

32. Berry, "Manifesto: The Mad Farmer Liberation Front," *The Mad Farmer Poems* (Berkeley: Counterpoint Press, 2014), 19.

33. Valarie Kaur, *See No Stranger: A Memoir and Manifesto of Revolutionary Love* (London: One World, 2020), 307.

in the face of what is most painful and most broken in our lives and the world.

Finding God in all things is what sustains us in gratitude, joy, delight, and beauty for the long journey of faith. Gratitude, joy, delight, and beauty are God's gifts, moment-by-moment sacramental reminders, that nothing "in all creation will be able to separate us from the love of God that is in Christ Jesus our Lord" (Romans 8:39).

Trouble today, trouble tomorrow, Jesus promised us. *Count on it. Don't be surprised when trouble comes knocking. But, because I have overcome the world, you can too* (see John 16:33). Amen.

FOR REFLECTION

- How can we develop the habit and skill of noticing that the whole earth is full of the glory of God?
- Pick one of the five senses—sight, taste, touch, smell, hearing—and see how it leads you to experience God's love in a new and transforming way this week.
- Take a picture every day for a month of something that represents beauty to you. You can keep it to yourself or share it with others. See how this practice strengthens the grip of resilience in your life.
- Notice how many different birds you can hear and see on a walk outside. Anne Lamott joyfully observes of birds: "Those little show-offs with their pure piping song can be the morning's reset button."[34]
- How can we remain attentive to God's presence even when there are no literal burning bushes?
- What have been some stepping stones to holiness in your life?

---

34. Lamott, *Almost Everything*, 178.

- How is God attending to, speaking to, wooing, or directing you through the ordinary, mundane, routine events and relationships of your life?
- The ability to see the sacred in the ordinary is a cultivated habit of sight. In light of this, what relationships or activities of your daily life can you begin to view through a sacramental lens?
- How can you cultivate the habit of gratitude in the midst of unfavorable circumstances?
- What people, places, and practices fill up your joy reservoir?

CONCLUSION

Resilient to the End

RESILIENCE TIP

Resilient people learn to see the Christian life as a moment-by-moment, three-steps-forward-two steps-back, lifelong process of drawing on the never-ceasing resources of God to persevere in the face of overwhelming circumstances so they can in turn be a vital source of faith, hope, love, peace, and joy to others in the midst of their pain and injustice.

> *"But where shall I find courage?" asked Frodo. "That is what I chiefly need."*
> *"Courage is found in unlikely places," said Gildor.*
> —*J. R. R. Tolkien,* The Fellowship of the Ring

> *We have to fight daily, like fleas, those many small worries about the morrow, for they sap our energies. . . . The things that have to be done must be done, and for the rest we must not allow ourselves to become infested with thousands of petty fears and worries, so many motions of no confidence in God. Ultimately, we have just one moral duty: to reclaim large areas of peace in ourselves, more and more peace, and reflect it toward others. And the more peace there is in us, the more peace there will also be in our troubled world.*
> —*Etty Hillesum,* An Interrupted Life and Letters from Westerbork

> *At night, as I lay in the camp on my plank bed, surrounded by women and girls gently snoring, dreaming aloud, quietly sobbing and tossing*

and turning, women and girls who often told me during the day, "We don't want to think, we don't want to feel, otherwise we are sure to go out of our minds," I was sometimes filled with an infinite tenderness, and lay awake for hours letting all the many, too many impressions of a much-too-long day wash over me, and I prayed, "Let me be the thinking heart of these barracks."

—*Etty Hillesum*, An Interrupted Life
and Letters from Westerbork

God's invitation to each of us is to grasp "the life that is truly life" (1 Timothy 6:19) by becoming the kind of people who flourish in Christlike holiness in the midst of the setbacks and storms of life. None of us is born pre-loaded with resilience. Resilience is not a divine zap that effortlessly pushes obstacles out of the way or instantly makes us immune to trials and temptations. Resilience takes practice, one moment, one day at a time. God gives us grace, but we also need to flex our faith muscles. Resilience grows gradually as we respond to the temptations, trials, disappointments, and failures of a lifetime. Resilience is the commitment to pray as if life totally depends on God and to work as if it all depends on us. It is "a long obedience in the same direction."[1] It's a long faithfulness in loving God and our neighbors.

Resilience is showing up every day, rain or shine, when we feel like it and when we don't. It is three steps forward and two steps back. When we fall, it's dusting ourselves off and getting back on the journey. It's being "in season out of season" (2 Timothy 4:2). It's throwing off whatever is slowing us down or tripping us up (Hebrews 12:1). It's building character one day, one decision at a time. It's creating micro-practices, weaving small changes and healthy habits into the fabric of our daily lives. These practices

---

1. See Eugene Peterson, *A Long Obedience in the Same Direction: Discipleship in an Instant Society* (Grand Rapids: IVP, 2021).

are not heroic or life-changing in and of themselves, but little by little, thread by thread, we begin to weave a more Christlike, more resilient fabric of life.

Resilient people are flexible in responding to the obstacles of life. They have learned to manage high levels of stress. They stay attentive to the fuel gauge of their life, making sure there is as much life flowing into them as out of them. They experience seasons of doubt, embracing challenges to their faith as creative opportunities to know God more intimately. They tend to their spiritual keel so that, when storms of adversity blow into their lives, they are able to right themselves and stay on course. They grow tired and become exhausted but are committed to getting regular, adequate sleep so their bodies and emotions receive the rest needed to rejuvenate.

Resilient people are on the journey of a lifetime. They continue to plant seeds of faithfulness even when there is no visible fruit to their efforts. They experience seemingly insurmountable obstacles, but they keep praying, trusting, waiting, and searching for creative solutions. They experience feelings of depression, anxiety, anger, frustration, and fear but embrace the means of grace God provides for the healing of trauma and wounded emotions: counseling, medical help, prayer, and the body of Christ. Because they are able to maintain hope in the midst of painful circumstances, they are able in turn to offer compassionate hope to others who are hurting. Resilient people learn to find God in all things so that their lives are lived from a vital spring of gratitude, beauty, joy, and delight even in the face of difficult circumstances.

Etty Hillesum

In my own attempts to remain resilient, I find myself drawn to the stories of those who have faced the worst that life can dish out yet have remained resilient and faithful. If they can do it, then I can too. And so can you.

I want to end this book by telling the story of one of the more recent and important mentors in my life, Etty Hillesum.[2] Her life and witness help keep me steady when the storms of life threaten to blow me off course.

Etty was a young Jewish woman who lived in Amsterdam when World War II began. She was a deep thinker and budding writer. She kept a regular journal and wrote many letters to friends and family that have been collected and published in English translation only within the last two or three decades.[3] As conditions worsened in western Europe in the late 1930s, there was much for her to worry about. She watched carefully as the Nazis invaded and occupied the Netherlands in May 1940. She and her family, along with thousands of other Jewish families throughout Holland, were eventually forced to relocate to Camp Westerbork, a Nazi transit camp in northern Holland.[4]

Etty's path to faith in Christ was unusual. As a Jew, she obviously did not attend a Christian church, but a friend gave her a Bible and some other Christian books that she eagerly devoured. Through her Bible reading, introspection, and personal prayer life, she came to develop a relationship with Christ. In reading her journals, it becomes clear rather quickly that her overflowing life with God made it possible for her to withstand the dehumanization and despair of concentration-camp life. Three months before her death in Auschwitz, she wrote to a friend about how her life with God sustained her during such overwhelming times:

> You have made me so rich, oh God, please let me share out your beauty with open hands. My life has become an uninterrupted

2. I feel like Etty has indeed become a personal friend. It seems only fitting to refer to her by her first name.

3. To the impoverishment of us all, Etty's journals were not even published in Dutch until 1981, almost forty years after her death.

4. Westerbork is the same transit camp where Anne Frank and her family were imprisoned before being transferred to Auschwitz. If you are ever in Holland, I highly recommend visiting Camp Westerbork and the Anne Frank House. They are heartbreaking but necessary visits.

dialogue with you, oh God, one great dialogue. Sometimes when I stand in some corner of the camp, my feet planted on your earth, my eyes raised toward your heaven, tears sometimes run down my face, tears of deep emotion and gratitude. At night, too, when I lie in my bed and rest in you, oh God, tears of gratitude run down my face, and that is my prayer. . . . Things come and go in a deeper rhythm, and people must be taught to listen; it is the most important thing we have to learn in this life. . . . The beat of my heart has grown deeper, more active, and yet more peaceful, and it is as if I were all the time storing up inner riches.[5]

Her life with God was a lively stream that helped insulate her against the violence and stresses she faced daily in Camp Westerbork.

It was no secret to Etty and many others in Holland what was going on in the Nazi concentration camps in eastern Europe. Just a few days before she and her family were forced into Westerbork, she wrote of drawing strength from Jesus's words in Matthew 6:34. In the midst of the gathering Nazi storm, Jesus's words reminded her not to worry:

We have to fight daily, like fleas, those many small worries about the morrow, for they sap our energies. . . . The things that have to be done must be done, and for the rest we must not allow ourselves to become infested with thousands of petty fears and worries, so many motions of no confidence in God. Ultimately, we have just one moral duty: to reclaim large areas of peace in ourselves, more and more peace, and reflect it toward others. And the more peace there is in us, the more peace there will also be in our troubled world.[6]

Living under the ever-encroaching shadow of evil, Etty realized that if she were to stay rooted in God, she had to dig beneath

---

5. Etty Hillesum, *An Interrupted Life and Letters from Westerbork* (New York: Metropolis Books, 1996), 332.

6. Hillesum, *An Interrupted Life*, 218.

the daily horrors and draw from an ongoing vital source. The presence of God's peace and love in ourselves, she says, ripples out into the rest of the world in both visible and invisible ways. Etty understood that, without a sense that life is truly sacred and beautiful, we will find it difficult to hope and live a life of love in the kind and gentle ways that truly can heal the deep woundedness of this life.

The experience of beauty sustained her both before and during the miseries of concentration-camp life. Before her imprisonment in Westerbork, she stopped one night in the rain with a blister on her foot to look for a flower stall. She took home with her a large bouquet of roses. She wrote of their beauty, "And there they are. They are just as real as all the misery I witness each day."[7] She was aware that she needed to fill herself with as much beauty as possible to steel herself against the coming storm.

Another time music filled her inner reservoir with the strength to sustain her during the awful days to come:

> This afternoon during the Beethoven, I suddenly had to bow my head and pray for all those who are lingering in freezing concentration camps, prayed God to give them strength to remember the good moments of their lives, just as in hard times I shall remember this day and many days during the last year, and draw what strength I need from them lest I become embittered with life. We must see to it that we daily grow in strength to bear the times that will come.[8]

Because of her sense of God's nearness, even in the valley of the shadow of death, Etty was able to rest in the assurance that her life was beloved. Only a life firmly rooted in God's love and the hope of Christ and lived in the divine flow of the Holy Spirit could have endured such evils. Sensing herself as "beloved,

---

7. Quoted in Patrick Woodhouse, *Etty Hillesum: A Life Transformed* (New York: Bloomsbury, 2019), 71.

8. Woodhouse, *Etty Hillesum*, 72.

cherished, and made beautiful by God,"[9] she was able to keep extending love to those who were overwhelmed by the wretchedness of Westerbork. Her joyful spirit and helpfulness were known throughout the camp. Even so, she did not deny or minimize the pain she felt:

> The misery here is quite terrible; yet, late at night when the day has slunk away from the depths behind me, I often walk with a spring in my step along the barbed wire. And then time and again, it soars straight from my heart—I can't help it, that's just the way it is, like some elementary force—the feeling that life is glorious and magnificent, and that one day we shall be building a whole new world. Against every new outrage and every fresh horror, we shall put up one more piece of love and goodness, drawing strength from within ourselves. We may suffer, but we must not succumb.[10]

Etty's resilience in the face of her own pain in Westerbork is remarkable. Before her imprisonment, she had many opportunities to go into hiding, but she chose to remain with family and friends, to share their pain and lighten the heavy burdens they carried. She could have hated, but she kept loving. She could have despaired, but she continued to hope. As Norman Wirzba observes, Etty "turned her life into a human vessel for the receiving and sharing of God's love. To the very end, her life was a daily exercise of gentleness and kindness shown to others."[11]

Anticipating the worst yet to come, Etty wrote in her last journal entry, "Today will be a hard day. I shall lie quietly and try to anticipate something of all the hard days that are to come." She concluded her journal resolved to keep working for God's new world: "We should be willing to act as a balm for all wounds."[12]

---

9. Wirzba, *This Sacred Life*, 254.
10. Hillesum, *An Interrupted Life*, 294.
11. Wirzba, *This Sacred Life*, 254.
12. Hillesum, *An Interrupted Life*, 230–231.

Those who saw Etty board an overcrowded freight car bound for Auschwitz on September 7, 1943, said she left singing. In a postcard written to a friend and thrown from the train as it left Westerbork, Etty wrote, "Opening the Bible at random I find this: 'The Lord is my high tower.' I am sitting on my rucksack in the middle of a full freight car."[13] Her friend Jopie Vleeschhouwer wrote to family and friends of Etty's last moments in Westerbork: "Talking gaily, smiling, a kind word for everyone she met on the way, full of sparkling humor, perhaps just a touch of sadness, but every inch the Etty you all know so well."[14] Etty Hillesum was murdered in the Auschwitz death camp on November 30, 1943. She was twenty-nine. She remained a faithful witness to the end.

Etty's faithfulness provokes our theological imagination to consider the kind of life that a life rooted in God makes possible. None of us can ever know how we would have lived during similar circumstances. The only evidence for the kind of person we can become by the grace of God is how we live our lives each moment of every day in exactly the place we find ourselves in this present moment. We might wish we were somewhere else instead of here, but it is precisely here that we are called to live faithfully the life we've been given to live. *How will we respond to the adversities of life? What kind of people are we becoming by the grace of God and our intentional, consistent effort? When all the veneer and external trappings of life are peeled back, who are we, really? What character does our life display? How are our deepest commitments to extend the compassion and love of Christ expressed in our lives?*

The witness of Etty's life to God's love, kindness, joy, and beauty in the midst of the misery of Camp Westerbork and the anticipated suffering in Auschwitz is compelling. She understood that it was impossible for her to go on living in Hitler's concentration camps without the sense of hope that God's nearness brings. Etty

---

13. Hillesum, *An Interrupted Life*, 360. The postcard was found by farmers on the ground outside Westerbork.

14. Hillesum, *An Interrupted Life*, 364.

embodied and gave voice to what we referred to in the last chapter as "finding God in all things." That God is active and present in all things does not mean God causes sickness, death, war, or evil but that God is active and present to renew, redeem, and reconcile all things in Christ, even in the worst circumstances imaginable.

Etty's life exemplifies the character traits we've highlighted throughout this book. Her life was rooted in God's unconditional love for her, and she extended God's love to others. A vital prayer life gave her the courage to pray, "Let me be the thinking heart of this barracks." She went on to write of the vital lifeline of prayer in her life: "One ought to pray, day and night, for the thousands. . . . Alone for once in the middle of the night, God and I have been left together, and I feel all the richer for it."[15]

Living a life of faithful love for the sake of others led her to be concerned with the needs and miseries of others when attending to her own needs would have been easier. Her vibrant relationship with God, nurtured in prayer and Scripture, helped her maintain a sense of God's redemptive work and presence even in a Nazi concentration camp. Because of her deep faith, she embodied a life of Christlike resilience as she continued to see God's presence reflected in beauty, joy, and gratitude. Etty viewed it as God's call on her life to witness to what she and too many others experienced at the hands of the Nazis. Like Corrie and Betsie ten Boom, she understood that her journal would continue to speak when she herself no longer could: "Yet there must be someone to live through it all and bear witness to the fact that God lived, even in these times."[16]

Our hope as Christ followers is that, in the worst of times, God is at work. God's love remains even in the face of the most despicable of human evils. Michael Lodahl speaks of this very thing in *The Story of God* when he affirms, "The Spirit was in

---

15. Hillesum, *An Interrupted Life*, 225, 226.
16. Hillesum, *Etty: The Letters and Diaries of Etty Hillesum, 1941–1943* (Grand Rapids: Eerdmans, 2002), 506.

Auschwitz's fiery pits of burning children, in the eye-melting heat of the Hiroshima blast—and most particularly, hanging on the cross of Jesus."[17] Etty and the apostle Paul stand as witnesses to God's faithfulness, affirming that there is nothing in all creation that can snatch us from the love of God revealed in Jesus Christ our Lord. I pray that Paul's words strengthen the grip of the resilience of Christ in your life as they have in mine over the years: "No, in all these things we are more than victorious through him who loved us. For I am convinced that neither death, nor life, nor angels, nor rulers, nor things present, nor things to come, nor powers, nor height, nor depth, nor anything else in all creation will be able to separate us from the love of God in Christ Jesus our Lord (Romans 8:37–39, NRSVUE).

God bless you and your loved ones as you travel on the long and sometimes painful road of resilience. You are not alone.

FOR REFLECTION

- What stuck out to you most about Etty's life, and why?
- Imagine living in a concentration camp. What would sustain you?
- What practices of resilience can you begin building into your life to fill up your internal reservoir so you are better prepared for whatever storms come?
- What makes a life like Etty's possible? What makes it possible for you to live a life of Christlike resilience?
- Who are your mentors, past and present, who give you the courage and hope to persevere in the face of pain, illness, failure, or loss?

---

17. Lodahl, *The Story of God*, 62.

- Consider copying one of Etty's statements included in this chapter and putting it in your Bible or another place where you have opportunity to reflect on it.

ACKNOWLEDGMENTS

Just as authors write the books they need to read, no author ever writes a book alone.

If it weren't for the longsuffering of the good folk at Golden Church of the Nazarene in Colorado, I might not have persisted long enough in ministry to begin teaching and writing. I express my heartfelt gratitude in particular to Paul and Margaret Dodson, Steve and Debbie Smith, Joann and Marv Carlson, and the Schoech family.

Thank you to my editor, Audra Spiven at The Foundry Publishing, for your careful attention to detail and wise insights that have made this a stronger book.

Thank you to my colleagues and students in the College of Theology and Christian Ministry at Northwest Nazarene University for a fun and creative place in which to teach and write.

Thank you to my special friends-become-family in Africa who have sustained my family and me through their love and prayers during some difficult times: Celestin and Esperance Chishibanji, Democratic Republic of the Congo; Frank and Hannah Mills, Ghana; Simone Pierre and Caritas Rwaramba, Rwanda.

Thank you to my mother, Linda Tague, for unconditional love and unflagging support.

Thank you to my adult children, Jimmie and Annie, daughter-in-law, Leslie, and granddaughter, Quincy, for lots of love and laughter.

Thank you to my partner in life and in resilience—my wife and best friend, Shelly. I would never have written this book without you at my side. I love exploring life with you!

NOTES

The full bibliographic information for the epigraphs in each chapter can be found here.

Alighieri, Dante. *The Inferno of Dante: A New Verse Translation by Robert Pinsky.* "Canto I." New York: Noonday Press, 1994.

Andrew, Mari. *My Inner Sky: On Embracing Day, Night, and All the Times in Between.* New York: Penguin Books, 2021.

Berry, Wendell. *Standing by Words: Essays.* Berkeley, CA: Counterpoint Press, 1983.

Berry, Wendell. *The Selected Poems of Wendell Berry.* Washington, DC: Counterpoint Press, 1998.

Bethke, Jefferson. *Jesus > Religion: Why He Is So Much Better Than Trying Harder, Doing More, and Being Good Enough.* Nashville: Nelson Books, 2013.

Buechner, Frederick. *Listening to Your Life: Daily Meditations with Frederick Buechner.* New York: HarperCollins, 1992.

Buechner, Frederick. *Wishful Thinking: A Theological ABC.* New York: HarperCollins, 1993.

Frankl, Viktor. *Man's Search for Meaning.* Boston: Beacon Press, 2006.

Hillesum, Etty. *An Interrupted Life and Letters from Westerbork.* New York: Metropolis Books, 1997.

Hopkins, Gerard Manley. *Gerard Manley Hopkins: Selected Poems.* Edited by Bob Blaisdell. Mineola, NY: Dover, 2011.

Iona Community. *Iona Abbey Worship Book.* Glasgow, UK: Wild Goose Publications, 2001.

Lamott, Anne. *Almost Everything: Notes on Hope.* New York: Riverhead Books, 2018.

L'Engle, Madeleine. *Two-Part Invention: The Story of a Marriage.* San Francisco: HarperSanFrancisco, 1989.

Lodahl, Michael. *The Story of God: A Narrative Theology.* Kansas City, MO: Beacon Hill Press of Kansas City, 2008.

Loehr, Jim and Tony Schwartz. *The Power of Full Engagement: Managing Energy, Not Time, Is the Key to High Performance and Personal Renewal*. New York: Simon & Schuster, 2003.

Mackesy, Charlie. *The Boy, the Mole, the Fox and the Horse*. San Francisco: HarperOne, 2019.

Manning, Brennan. *Abba's Child: The Cry of the Heart for Intimate Belonging*. Colorado Springs: NavPress, 2002.

Miles, Sara. *Jesus Freak: Feeding, Healing, Raising the Dead*. London: Canterbury Press, 2012.

Nouwen, Henri J. M. *Life of the Beloved: Spiritual Living in a Secular World*. New York: Crossroad Publishing Company, 2002.

O'Donohue, John. *To Bless the Space between Us: A Book of Blessings*. New York: Convergent Books, 2008.

Ó Tuama, Pádraig. *Daily Prayer with the Corrymeela Community*. London: Canterbury Press, 2017.

Oliver, Mary. *Devotions: The Selected Poems of Mary Oliver*. New York: Penguin Press, 2017.

Saint Thérèse of Lisieux. *The Story of a Soul: The Autobiography of the Little Flower*. Wolfville, Nova Scotia: Anthony Clark Books, 1973.

Starr, Mirabai. *The Showings of Julian of Norwich: A New Translation*. Charlottesville, VA: Hampton Roads, 2013.

Tolkien, J. R. R. *The Fellowship of the Ring: Being the First Part of The Lord of the Rings*. Boston: Houghton Mifflin, 1988.

Wesley, John. *The Works of John Wesley*. Edited by Thomas Jackson. Third edition. Kansas City, MO: Beacon Hill Press of Kansas City, 1979.

Wolterstorff, Nicholas. *Lament for a Son*. Grand Rapids: Eerdmans, 1987.